T0328762

Cambridge Elements ≡

Elements in Experimental Political Science
edited by
James N. Druckman
Northwestern University

MACHINE LEARNING FOR EXPERIMENTS IN THE SOCIAL SCIENCES

Jon Green
Northeastern University

Mark H. White II
Etsy, Inc.

CAMBRIDGE
UNIVERSITY PRESS

Shaftesbury Road, Cambridge CB2 8EA, United Kingdom

One Liberty Plaza, 20th Floor, New York, NY 10006, USA

477 Williamstown Road, Port Melbourne, VIC 3207, Australia

314–321, 3rd Floor, Plot 3, Splendor Forum, Jasola District Centre, New Delhi – 110025, India

103 Penang Road, #05–06/07, Visioncrest Commercial, Singapore 238467

Cambridge University Press is part of Cambridge University Press & Assessment, a department of the University of Cambridge.

We share the University's mission to contribute to society through the pursuit of education, learning and research at the highest international levels of excellence.

www.cambridge.org
Information on this title: www.cambridge.org/9781009168229

DOI: 10.1017/9781009168236

First published 2023

A catalogue record for this publication is available from the British Library.

ISBN 978-1-009-16822-9 Paperback
ISSN 2633-3368 (online)
ISSN 2633-335X (print)

Machine Learning for Experiments in the Social Sciences

Elements in Experimental Political Science

DOI: 10.1017/9781009168236
First published online: March 2023

Jon Green
Northeastern University

Mark H. White II
Etsy, Inc.

Author for correspondence: Jon Green, jo.green@northeastern.edu

Abstract: Causal inference and machine learning are typically introduced in the social sciences separately as theoretically distinct methodological traditions. However, applications of machine learning in causal inference are increasingly prevalent. This Element provides theoretical and practical introductions to machine learning for social scientists interested in applying such methods to experimental data. We show how machine learning can be useful for conducting robust causal inference and provide a theoretical foundation researchers can use to understand and apply new methods in this rapidly developing field. We then demonstrate two specific methods – the prediction rule ensemble and the causal random forest – for characterizing treatment effect heterogeneity in survey experiments and testing the extent to which such heterogeneity is robust to out-of-sample prediction. We conclude by discussing the limitations and tradeoffs of such methods, while directing readers to additional related methods available on the Comprehensive R Archive Network (CRAN).

Keywords: experiments, machine learning, causal inference, social science, treatment effects

ISBNs: 9781009168229 (PB), 9781009168236 (OC)
ISSNs: 2633-3368 (online), 2633-335X (print)

Supplementary materials for this Element can be found at:
http://www.cambridge.org/GreenWhiteII

Contents

1 Introduction

Causal inference and machine learning are both widespread methodological approaches in the social sciences. Each emerged largely independent of the other, and social scientists tend to view the two approaches as useful for addressing fundamentally different research questions. Causal inference – the randomized experiment in particular – is the gold standard for testing hypothesized mechanisms, prioritizing theory and interpretability. By contrast, researchers tend to prefer machine learning when the goal is to make useful predictions, interpretability is less important, or theoretical expectations are not clear at the outset. As such, social scientists have tended to avoid machine learning methods when they are interested in theory building, hypothesis testing, and causal identification.

However, the divide between causal inference and machine learning has narrowed in recent years. Recently developed methods now allow social scientists to apply the core principles of machine learning to questions concerning causal inference. Not only are these tools powerful for testing theories; they are also powerful for building theories, expanding the scope of feasible social science research and our knowledge of the social world.

These methodological advances are important in their own right, but they also invite a more fundamental reconsideration of the theoretical distinction between causal inference and machine learning – and, by extension, between explanation and prediction (Hoffman, Sharma, and Watts 2021). Many of the core concepts and principles from each approach add value to our understanding of the other. Many causal hypotheses, for example, are well-understood as *predictions* about the relationships between social phenomena. By the same token, recent issues in causal inference concerning replication and reproducible research are well-understood from the perspective of machine learning as a problem of inaccurate out-of-sample predictions.

This Element provides a practical introduction to the key theories and core current methods at the intersection of machine learning and causal inference. It will bridge the two methodological traditions, highlighting the commonalities between them and approaching causal hypotheses from the perspective of making good predictions. It will also provide working examples and code – relying on the open-source R programming language – for both basic machine learning analyses and methods that systematically explore variation in experimental treatment effects.[1]

---

[1] To preserves space and keep the focus on experimental methods, much of the code for basic machine learning analyses can be found in the supporting materials (https://osf.io/paxhs/) rather than the text of this Element itself.

This Element will be most useful to advanced undergraduates, graduate students, and faculty in the social sciences. We assume a basic familiarity with causal inference – particularly experiments – though we briefly review the potential outcomes framework in the next section. We also assume a basic familiarity with R, which we use for all demonstrations and applications here. We do not assume any prior familiarity with machine learning.

1.1 Why This Element?

Practically speaking, what does machine learning contribute to our ability to learn from experiments? That is, let's say we relax the theoretical distinction between causal inference's emphasis on explanation and machine learning's emphasis on prediction. *So what?* Why is machine learning useful for an experimental social scientist to add to their toolkit?

We see two main and related reasons. First, machine learning provides frameworks for conducting exploratory research in a reproducible manner. Second, and more specifically, machine learning provides tools for systematically identifying treatment effect heterogeneity and the extent to which such heterogeneity is robust to out-of-sample prediction. We elaborate on both of these points in Sections 1.1.1 and 1.1.2 and in subsequent sections.

1.1.1 Reproducible Exploration

Much of social science relies on conducting exploratory analyses, in which researchers test for the existence of interesting patterns in their data without strong theoretical expectations. Exploratory analyses can be extremely useful in social science. The social world is complex, and we often cannot anticipate in advance all of the interesting relationships lurking in our data. As such, exploratory analyses can be important for developing theoretical expectations that can be subsequently tested in confirmatory analyses.

While exploratory research can be incredibly valuable, it can be tempting to conduct exploratory research in a haphazard, non-systematic manner. This risks generating results that fail to generalize beyond one's own data. In order for a result to teach us something about the social world, we need to be confident that it is not an idiosyncratic quirk attributable to you or your specific data. We need to be confident that if we set out to answer the same research question under similar conditions, we would *reproduce* your answer.

The principles and tools of machine learning can help researchers conduct systematic explorations of their data in ways that involve fewer decisions that may influence eventual findings. As we discuss in Section 3, machine learning's emphasis on out-of-sample prediction means that reproducibility is included as a criterion used to evaluate patterns identified in the data. This means that even (and perhaps especially) when we do not have strong theoretical expectations regarding the patterns we expect to find in our data, and therefore prefer to let such patterns emerge from systematic exploration, machine learning can be useful for helping ensure that we conduct such exploration in a reproducible manner.

1.1.2 Treatment Effect Heterogeneity

Conducting reproducible research is important in general, but for experimental social scientists it is especially important when characterizing heterogeneity in treatment effects. Experimental social scientists are frequently interested in treatment effect heterogeneity (i.e., moderators), and with good reason. In theory, we know that while a randomized experiment's average treatment effect is unbiased, it does not precisely describe the effect the treatment has on each individual. Put simply, all treatment effects vary. The question is therefore not whether they vary but whether this variation is systematic and statistically identifiable. Moreover, it is crucial to understand the potential for treatment effect heterogeneity before acting on an experiment's results in a real-world setting (Bryan, Tipton, and Yeager 2021). In practice, "when does the treatment work?" and "for whom does the treatment work?" can be as important as "does the treatment work?"

However, identifying the extent to which variation in treatment effects is systematic and robust to new data is difficult, even under the best circumstances. It is virtually impossible when the analyses producing evidence of such heterogeneity are not conducted in a reproducible manner. In recent years, social science has, as a discipline, developed a variety of tools for ensuring that treatment effect heterogeneity is more reproducible. In particular, new norms regarding preregistering hypotheses and analysis plans help ensure that, at the very least, significant subgroup differences were not the product of post hoc "fishing" expeditions.

The methodological framework provided by machine learning, with its emphasis on out-of-sample prediction, is particularly well-suited to systematically characterizing effect heterogeneity in a reproducible manner. First, its methods tend to emphasize modeling individual-level sensitivity to a treatment over quantifying the uncertainty around a specific interaction term. Second, its key standard of evaluation is whether these individual-level estimates of sensitivity to treatment are useful for predicting outcomes in new data that were not used to estimate such sensitivity. That is, the machine learning workflow can be thought of as including both exploratory and confirmatory stages of analysis.

1.2 Goals of This Element

We hope that readers come away from this Element with two types of understanding about machine learning for experiments in the social sciences. The first is *transferable* knowledge. The field of machine learning for causal inference is rapidly growing, with new methodologies emerging on a regular basis. As scholars continue to advance the field of machine learning for causal inference with new statistical packages and academic articles, the theoretical motivation and conceptual background in Sections 4 and 5 should allow readers to feel comfortable approaching, understanding, and applying these new methods. The second is *specific* knowledge. The tutorials we provide for prediction rule ensembles (Section 6) and causal random forests (Section 7) aim to provide practical introductions to these methodologies so that social scientists can use them in their research. In short, this Element will teach you how to use a few specific tools, but it should also enable you to teach yourself new tools as they are developed and popularized.

1.3 Outline

Section 2 introduces causal inference through the lens of potential outcomes. We chose this theoretical framework for causal inference because it complements the theoretical underpinnings of machine learning—based approaches. Perhaps for this reason, in our read of the literature on machine learning for causal inference, the potential outcomes framework is the most common theoretical foundation. We hope that the introduction here allows readers to go on to read this body of literature with an understanding of what people mean when they say potential outcomes and how the potential outcomes framework can serve as a bridge between explanatory claims and predictive claims. Readers who are already familiar with the potential outcomes framework for causal inference may choose to skim or skip this section, but it is important to establish this common ground on which the rest of the Element builds.

Section 3 moves on to discussing an apparent "crisis" in social science of published findings not being able to be replicated by other researchers. We review this "crisis" and ways that researchers are reacting to it. We then discuss how proposed solutions undercut the importance of exploratory research. We argue that a balance can be found, such that researchers can do exploratory analysis in a responsible and principled way. We introduce machine learning methods as one way to do this.

Section 4 thus focuses on introducing social scientists to key concepts in machine learning: the bias-variance tradeoff, held-out data and cross-validation, regularization, tree-based methods, and ensembles. We try to cover these at a conceptual level, providing readers with citations to the deeper mathematical texts to read after they have a basic understanding.

Section 5 explicitly links machine learning concepts (e.g., held-out validation and regularization) to reproducible research in the social sciences. We discuss a growing field in machine learning that is focused on identifying heterogeneous treatment effects. We pay special attention to how these methods can help encourage exploration while providing a principled, systematic way to do so – that is, without relying on researcher degrees of freedom and "fishing" for significant p-values.

Sections 6 and 7 introduce two machine learning methods for learning about varying treatment effects. Prediction rule ensembles (Section 6) combine tree-based methods with penalized regression to generate interpretable rules describing variation in treatment effects. Causal random forests (Section 7) explicitly focus on identifying treatment effect variation to generate predicted effects at the individual level. These tutorials will draw on principles discussed in previous sections, and provide code, such that readers can apply these methods in their own work.

Section 8 wraps up the Element. We restate our goals and summarize what we have covered. Lastly, we discuss limitations to these approaches, as they are certainly not a panacea for the problems facing the social sciences. And there is no free lunch: We also discuss the costs of using these methods.

2 Causal Inference

Much of social science, for both scholars and practitioners, involves identifying generalizable patterns in the social world. Causal inference is crucial in this endeavor. To gain a better understanding of how the world works, and how we can make it better, we often want to know whether and how changing something causes changes in something else.

One reason (of many) why causal inference is important is because it can allow us to generalize identified causal mechanisms into *predictions*. When we understand whether and how changing something caused changes in something else, we may be able to predict that similar changes *will cause* similar effects in similar settings. To say that people update their attitudes in response to stimuli in an attempt to maintain consistency – a core principle of Balance Theory in psychology (Heider 1958; Crandall et al. 2007) – is to predict that, for example, Democrats *will feel* more warmly toward a certain type of architecture after being told that an unpopular Republican strongly dislikes it (Blair 2020). Practically, it is useful for political consultants to know whether a particular campaign tactic caused more people to vote because they want to know whether that tactic will cause similar people to vote at higher rates in the future (Green and Gerber 2004). Causal inference allows us to make useful, informed, and falsifiable predictions about these future or unobserved events.

2.1 Potential Outcomes

There are many useful ways to conceptualize "causality" (Beebee, Hitchcock, and Menzies 2009), but we use what is often referred to as the "potential outcomes" framework or "Rubin's causal model" (Rubin 1974; Holland 1986) in this Element. This approach defines causality as a difference between two potential outcomes.

Consider the effect of consuming news media on mood. An individual is scrolling on their computer and either sees a political opinion piece written by someone with an opposing political ideology (let's call this a treatment with the value of 1) or does not see the article and continues on with their day (a lack of the treatment we can represent with 0). Let's call their mood Y, with higher values indicating better mood. Whether they see the article or not (i.e., levels of the "treatment" or "condition"), each has its own potential outcome. There is the value of the potential mood if this person sees the article, $Y(1)$, and there is the potential mood if they do not see the article, $Y(0)$. The difference between these two potential outcomes is the causal effect of seeing the article on mood for that individual, $Y(1) - Y(0)$.

Put into words, the causal effect is the difference between this person's mood if (a) they had seen the article and (b) they had not seen it. Note that we use the language "if they had seen" to make clear that these are *potential* outcomes. They represent possible states of the world. We like this approach because it is intuitive, and it is also the logic behind many methods we describe in this Element.

2.1.1 The "Fundamental Problem"

The "true" treatment effect concerns these potential outcomes. Imagine the individual sees the article and we measure their mood. Let's say it equals three on a scale from one to seven, $Y(1) = 3$. However, to identify the "true" treatment effect, we also need to know – but cannot observe – what their mood *would have been* if they had not seen the article, $Y(0)$. Since they saw the article, we cannot observe $Y(0)$, and we therefore cannot measure this "true" treatment effect.

This is what Holland (1986) calls the "fundamental problem of causal inference." We would need some type of science fiction technology to measure the true treatment effect. With such technology, we could measure the individual's mood in the timeline where they see the article, $Y(1) = 3$. And we could measure their mood again in the timeline where they do not, $Y(0) = 5$. We would then know that the causal effect of seeing the article on mood for that individual is $3 - 5 = -2$.

Given the constraints of physical space and linear time, we cannot do this in our reality. That's why this is the "fundamental" problem. One could measure mood twice: once before and once after seeing the article (a "within-subjects" or "repeated-measures" design). However, there could be carryover effects (measuring the participant's mood the first time could affect their response the second time), or it might not be logistically feasible. An elegant approximation of a solution to this problem is the randomized experiment.

2.2 Why Experiments?

Experiments cannot completely solve the fundamental problem of causal inference. That is, they cannot identify the "true" effect of a treatment for each individual. However, they provide an efficient alternative. Rather than focusing on the causal effect for each individual, which is unobservable, they allow us to identify the average causal effect across *all* units studied (e.g., people, neighborhoods, schools). Keeping with the previous example: Rather than having one individual see an article or not, we can instead randomly assign many individuals to either see an article or not. We can then measure all of their moods and compare the average mood in the group who saw the article to the average mood in the group who did not. We can't say for sure exactly how much seeing the article affected the mood of each individual who saw it (or would have affected the mood of each individual who didn't). But we can estimate how much seeing the article *tended* to affect mood across the group of individuals who saw it, compared to the group who didn't.

Let's say we do this for 100 individuals (Table 1). For each one, there is a potential outcome for Y in the timeline where they are shown the article and in the timeline where they aren't. These states of the world are represented in the parentheses next to Y. In Table 1, we can see potential outcomes for six of the participants. Remember that these are hypothetical, since we will not observe both outcomes for each person.

Each participant is then randomly assigned to either be shown the article or not (Table 2). This is denoted with its own variable, W, which can either be 1 or 0.

Table 1 Potential outcomes

Participant ID	Y(0)	Y(1)
1	3	6
2	2	5
3	5	7
. . .	. . .	. . .
98	4	5
99	6	6
100	4	6

Table 2 Potential outcomes with random assignment

Participant ID	Y(0)	Y(1)	W
1	3	6	0
2	2	5	0
3	5	7	1
. . .	. . .	. . .	. . .
98	4	5	1
99	6	6	1
100	4	6	0

Randomization provides us with a methodological tool (Rubin 2008) that allows us to meet assumptions necessary to calculate causal effects in a simple and intuitive way. The first assumption is what Holland (1986) calls the "independence assumption," or the assumption that our treatment assignment is otherwise unrelated to our independent or dependent variables. For example, randomization means that having a high value for $Y(0)$ is completely unrelated to whether $W = 0$ or $W = 1$. It also means that W is unrelated to any other variables correlated with Y. Randomized experiments are likely to meet this assumption and do not work without it. We must be able to assume that any systematic biases – such as confounding variables that might lead the two conditions to be different with regards to potential outcomes – have been rendered random.

The second assumption that must be met in order to identify the causal effect of our experiment is the stable unit treatment value assumption, or SUTVA. This allows us to assume that we are actually observing the potential outcomes associated with our treatment assignment, and it has two components. First, SUTVA requires the treatment to be the same across all respondents. When the treatment is being shown a specific article, this is fairly safe to assume, but sometimes it is not so straightforward. For example, randomly assigning respondents to exercise for a set amount of time may not satisfy SUTVA, as different individuals may choose different forms of exercise that vary in intensity (Hernàn and VanderWeele 2011). Being randomly assigned to exercise means different things to different individuals. Second, SUTVA stipulates that one unit's treatment status cannot affect other units' treatment status. This would be an issue in our hypothetical experiment here if, for example, an individual in our treatment group read the article and immediately sent it to an individual in our control group to tell them how angry it made them before we asked that control group respondent to report their mood. When we then observed their mood, we would incorrectly think that we were observing $Y(0)$ for them.

Now, consider the same table but with the two variables we actually observe: W and Y (Table 3). If W is 1, Y takes on the value of $Y(1)$; if W is 0, Y takes on the value of $Y(0)$. This reflects the fact that while each individual has two potential outcomes, we only observe the one corresponding to whether, in this timeline, they were randomly assigned to the treatment group.

Owing to the fundamental problem of causal inference, we can only observe $Y(1)$ or $Y(0)$ for each individual, so we cannot calculate the true treatment effects at the individual level. However, rather than asking what the true differences in outcomes are for each individual, we can ask ourselves what outcomes we could reasonably expect to observe for individuals who are either treated or not, and how these expectations differ, assuming that any individual-level differences will be random and cancel each other out. We can write this down in

Table 3 Potential and observed outcomes

Participant ID	$Y(0)$	$Y(1)$	W	Y
1	3	6	0	3
2	2	5	0	2
3	5	7	1	7
. . .	. . .	. . .	. . .	. . .
98	4	5	1	5
99	6	6	1	6
100	4	6	0	4

mathematical terms as $E(Y|W=1) - E(Y|W=0)$. E stands for the expected value, while the | represents a conditional statement (e.g., $E(Y|W=1)$ translates to "the expected value of Y when W equals 1").

2.2.1 Why Is This Useful?

When the assumptions are met, the difference in average outcomes between treatment and control groups is mathematically equivalent to the average of the (unobservable) individual differences in potential outcomes (Keele 2015). That is, this difference is an unbiased *estimate* of the *average* value of the true treatment effects (Rubin 1974). We call this the average treatment effect. In our example, we might observe that the average value of the outcome in the treatment condition is 6 and the average in the control condition is 3, for an average treatment effect of 3. From Table 3 – which lets us transcend time and space to observe multiple states of the world – we know that the true treatment effect of seeing the article for many individuals is not 3. However, based on what we can observe in the real world, our best guess as to the causal effect of seeing the article is the one we observe on average, 3.

2.2.2 When Is This Unsatisfying?

The average treatment effect is extremely useful. Without drawing on any additional information, and with a small set of assumptions that are easy to satisfy in our experimental context, the average treatment effect provides us with an unbiased approximation of our experimental treatment's effect on any individual in our study – regardless of whether they were assigned to the treatment or control condition. However, there are two reasons why we might not be satisfied with the average treatment effect on its own.

First, the average treatment effect we have generated in this example is just one estimate derived from a single attempt to identify the generalizable pattern in the social world in which we are interested (?). If we were to run the same study again, and again, and again, we might find much smaller differences in outcomes between our experimental conditions. It could have been the case that the difference we observed the first time was a fluke. That is, the finding may not be reproducible.

Second, the average treatment effect is an *overall* average, which we apply to every individual we studied. But we know that, in theory, the true treatment effect for each individual – the difference in their potential outcomes – is not always equal to that overall average. Some people are affected by the treatment more than the average, some less. If these differences are truly randomly distributed, we can ignore them: The overall average will remain our best guess as to the treatment effect for any individual. But we may suspect that the difference in potential outcomes between treatment and control condition will systematically differ based on some other observable characteristics about the individuals in our study. If we were able to identify those systematic differences in sensitivity to treatment, we would be able to make more precise claims about the nature of our experimental treatment effects. Replication and extension (i.e., finding moderators of the treatment effect) play a key role here in solidifying confidence in and understanding the mechanisms underlying causal processes. The methods presented in this Element allow researchers to systematically test for differences in sensitivity to experimental treatment effects while still remaining reproducible.

3 Exploratory and Reproducible Research

Social science is currently in the midst of a "crisis" – specifically, a "replication" or "reproducibility" crisis (Shrout and Rodgers 2018). That is, many findings that were widely accepted in their relevant fields of study have, when their associated experiments have been rerun, produced different (often null) results (Collaboration 2015; Ebersole et al. 2016; Klein et al. 2018; Klein et al. 2019; Ebersole et al. 2020).

Short of overt fraud, there are multiple possible reasons why a study might fail to replicate. The first, and most pejorative, is "p-hacking" (Simmons, Nelson, and Simonsohn 2011; Head et al. 2015). This describes cases when researchers perform selective data analysis strategies to obtain a p-value below the accepted standard (often 0.05). They may run the same experiment multiple times until they, by chance, find (and submit and publish) a result they want. They may drop "influential" cases that are deemed "outliers" after it is known that doing so will drop the p-value to below the threshold. They may run an experiment with five experimental conditions but only report the two that show significant effects. They may also run one experiment and haphazardly search for moderating variables until they find a significant interaction effect, again exploiting the statistical properties of null hypothesis significance testing to find low p-values to publish. And so on.

A second, more subtle reason why a study might fail to replicate is what Gelman and Loken (2013) call the "garden of forking paths." This refers to the fact that, given a particular dataset, different researchers may make different decisions regarding which observations to include, which covariates to consider, how to preprocess such data prior to analysis, and so on. These decisions can affect eventual results, even in the absence of intentional "p-hacking." Even given the same dataset, a series of individually defensible decisions can lead different researchers to draw different conclusions regarding a given research question (Silberzahn et al. 2018; Hoffman, Sharma, and Watts 2021).

Finally, biases can emerge during the publication pipeline. Editors and reviewers may be less inclined to publish null results, such that researchers perceive submitting a null result to be a waste of their time. This can create a "file drawer" problem where, for a given research question, the discipline does not observe the full distribution of answers (Rosenthal 1979).

3.1 Current Approaches for Reproducibility

As a discipline, social science has a variety of tools at its disposal to test (and improve) the generalizability of individual findings. For example, it is increasingly common to conduct studies where the unit of analysis is itself a study, comparing effect sizes found by many different researchers interested in similar questions, who may have made slightly different analytical or design decisions. This can include meta-analyses of effect sizes (Glass 1976), "p-curve" analyses to detect evidence of publication bias (Simonsohn, Nelson, and Simmons 2014), or "crowdsourced" analyses in which the same dataset is given to different research teams prior to publication (Silberzahn et al. 2018). Stronger norms and requirements regarding the availability of replication data and code – on which we will rely later in this Element – also make it easier for independent researchers to verify key claims made in published research or to extend such work on their own.

Finally, it is becoming increasingly common – and for some journals in the social sciences, required – for researchers to "pre-register" their studies (Nosek et al. 2018). Pre-registration involves writing down the core features of a study – such as what data will be collected, how it will be handled, and how it will be analyzed – before the study is conducted. This often involves explicitly stating one's research questions or hypotheses and how they will be tested. Analyses then proceed in accordance with the pre-registration, and authors are expected to note and justify any deviations from the pre-registration. This discourages researchers from generating post hoc hypotheses that conveniently fit relationships they already know exist in their data (Kerr 1998). In principle, this should lead to more replicable, generalizable findings. Preliminary evidence indicates that formally incorporating pre-registration into the publication process through "registered reports," in which a planned study is reviewed and accepted for publication prior to data collection and analysis, produces more rigorous and generally higher-quality work relative to the traditional publication process (Soderberg et al. 2021). There are many resources available to help make pre-registration easier for researchers and to host relevant documents anonymously for peer review, such as the EGAP Registry (egap.org), the Open Science Framework (osf.io), and AsPredicted (aspredicted.org).

3.2 The Problem of Irreproducible Research

Our research can and should be reproducible – especially when we are running experiments. When we are conducting this form of research, we are engaged in finding generalizable patterns in the social world. If independent researchers try and fail to reproduce a result, that can be a reason to be skeptical that the original finding generalizes.

Sometimes there are reasons for research to not be directly reproducible. It is not always possible to publish replication data when those data are proprietary, contain personal identifying information, or are protected by a website's terms of service, among other potential reasons. However, even in such cases, researchers should still be able to retrace your steps to have a clear understanding of how you came to find what you did, such that they could in principle conduct the same study themselves.

Research that is not reproducible – especially when it could have been – is uncertain. We are less sure whether the findings presented in irreproducible work represent generalizable patterns in the social world or if they are the product of some combination of researchers' decisions and random chance. Conducting research in ways that are not reproducible slows our disciplines' accumulation of knowledge.

3.3 The Importance of Exploratory Research

Often, all of the above is invoked so as to discourage researchers from conducting exploratory analyses – that is, analyzing collected data in search of interesting relationships without specific hypotheses in mind. This is generally sound advice: When not done in a systematic manner, exploratory research can often lead researchers to chase random noise. However, too heavy of an emphasis on practices such as pre-registration also has costs. In practice, they can tend to privilege well-resourced scholars who can afford to run multiple pilot studies before pre-registering and formally testing hypotheses. We may also waste valuable, hard-earned existing data by failing to explore relationships that may be important and generalizable but were not pre-registered.

More fundamentally, there may in fact be complex, nuanced causal relationships in one's data that are difficult to anticipate and systematically write down prior to analysis. In such cases, a heavy emphasis on pre-registration can risk penalizing researchers for not knowing the answers to their questions in advance (Rubin and Donkin 2022). Of course, if we always knew the answers to our research questions in advance, they wouldn't be interesting research questions. It is important for the social scientific community to preserve opportunities for exploratory research even as it moves toward making its research more reproducible.

In that spirit, we see no downside to researchers differentiating pre-registered from exploratory analyses when publishing their work – or in including the methods we outline in subsequent sections in pre-analysis plans. We simply note here that exploratory research has its own place in social science, as it can generate interesting results that are themselves useful for building new theories. Therefore, it is important to preserve opportunities for exploratory work in manners that are consistent with reproducible and generalizable research.

3.4 Finding a Balance

Counterintuitive as it may seem, exploratory and reproducible research are not necessarily at odds. Reported results can explicitly state which analyses were pre-registered and which were exploratory (or otherwise different from the pre-registration), so as to be transparent for the reader. However, while this is an improvement over exploratory research presented as if it were confirmatory, it is still subject to concerns regarding researcher degrees of freedom, gardens of forking paths, and so on. Still better would be to conduct exploratory research more systematically when such research is desirable and in ways that involve fewer decisions on the part of individual researchers.

This represents a key feature provided by machine learning methods. As we discuss in Section 4, one of the key features of machine learning is that it allows researchers to *systematically* explore data for relationships that are more likely to be *robust* to replication than traditional approaches. That said, the availability of these tools is not an excuse to avoid other best practices of reproducible research, such as pre-registering which variables will be considered for such exploratory analyses, how they will be preprocessed, if there are any criteria for excluding observations, and which specific methods will be applied (Ratkovic 2021). But, as we will elaborate on in the following sections, they provide researchers with the ability to conduct exploratory research in ways that are more likely to produce generalizable findings.

4 Machine Learning Basics

Machine learning has become an exciting, fashionable area of quantitative science in recent years, though precursors to some of its more popular methods extend back decades. As graduate students in political science and psychology, it was easy for us to feel intimidated by the buzz and see it as an "other" area of study, apart from the statistical training we were getting as social scientists. We aim to demystify key principles here.

We focus on *supervised machine learning* in this Element, as opposed to its *unsupervised* analogue. Supervised machine learning is the practice of using observed outputs (i.e., the dependent variable) and inputs (i.e., independent variables, covariates) to train a statistical model that "learns" to estimate the output from the set of inputs. This is in contrast with unsupervised learning, including methods such as clustering or topic modeling, where the outcomes are not observed in advance and therefore cannot "supervise" the process of learning relationships between inputs and outputs.

As a general equation, we can write supervised methods as: $Y = f(x) + \epsilon$ (James et al. 2013). Y is the output, x are the inputs, ϵ is an error term, and $f(x)$ is some function of the inputs that produces the output. This function represents the "data generating process," and the broad goal in supervised machine learning is to calculate an estimate of this function, $\hat{f}(x)$.

Ordinary least squares (OLS) regression is one method that does this. And indeed, OLS is commonly one of the earlier methods introduced in popular machine learning books as a foundation for understanding more complex supervised machine learning methods (Hastie, Tibshirani, and Friedman 2009; Kuhn and Johnson 2013; Burkov 2019; Géron 2019). However, many would not categorize OLS itself as machine learning because it does not incorporate additional features common to supervised machine learning methods that we introduce in this section.

It is beyond the scope of this Element to provide a comprehensive introduction to supervised machine learning. Instead, we aim to familiarize readers new to machine learning with concepts that will be central in applying supervised machine learning methods to experiments in the social sciences. For a user-friendly introduction to machine learning itself, we recommend James et al. (2013); for a detailed examination of the statistical theory underlying common machine learning methods, we recommend Hastie, Tibshirani, and Friedman (2009). For guidance on how to implement these methods in R under an approachable "tidy" framework, see Kuhn and Silge (2022).

4.1 Key Principles

4.1.1 Inference and Prediction

A key difference between classical statistics and machine learning is the goal of the researcher. Classical statistics are most useful for testing theory-driven hypotheses and making inferences. We run experiments and estimate $\hat{f}(x)$ to test null hypotheses based on our theories. Central to this is the appropriate calculation of standard errors, proper adjustments for p-values, and running well-powered experiments to minimize false positives and false negatives. The goal is to be able to make an inference about some larger social phenomena from the data, analyses, and results contained within a given study. We rarely take, for example, specific OLS coefficients in one study and feed data from another study into them to see how the estimated model performs on a different sample.

This practice is central to machine learning, which focuses on making useful predictions about unseen data not used to estimate $\hat{f}(x)$. Practitioners care less about the specific parameter estimates of particular independent variables in the given dataset they have, whether such parameters are statistically significant, or even about maximizing the amount of variation they can explain in the data they have at hand. Instead, they care more about estimating an $\hat{f}(x)$ that will make useful predictions. Machine learning places a greater emphasis on identifying patterns in observed data that are likely to generalize to new, unobserved data (Fariss and Jones 2018).

We distinguish "useful" predictions from "accurate" predictions because overall accuracy (i.e., "How many of our predictions were correct?") is not always the goal and can sometimes be misleading (Cranmer and Desmarais 2017). Consider a model for cancer screening. Cancer is relatively rare in the population as a whole at any particular moment, so a model that simply predicts that no one has cancer will be relatively "accurate." But, of course, such a model would also be completely useless. In this setting, Type I errors (incorrectly saying someone may have cancer) are less costly than Type II errors (missing a cancer diagnosis). One might estimate $\hat{f}(x)$ that is very sensitive (i.e., it picks up on the vast majority of cases where cancer is present) but not very precise (i.e., even if the prediction is "positive," one's likelihood of actually having cancer is still relatively low). Note here that while in some contexts researchers will be concerned with which specific observable indicators are "significantly" associated with cancer (and what it means about some given medical theory), that is less important here. The priority is diagnosing (i.e., predicting) as many cancer cases as possible.

This distinction between inference and prediction is instructive, but in practice it is too rigid (Shmueli 2010; Yarkoni and Westfall 2017). There are many contexts in which prediction informs inference, and vice versa. The extent to which a machine learning model's predictions are useful can itself be an interpretable quantity of interest. For example, the ability to predict the partisanship of a legislator based on their spoken or written words can be taken as an indicator of polarization, changes in this predictability over time can be informative of changes in how polarized a legislative body is, and identifying which words or phrases are most informative of speaker partisanship can indicate the substantive bases of such polarization (Peterson and Spirling 2018; Gentzkow, Shapiro, and Taddy 2019). Alternatively, establishing that we can predict with some degree of precision which individuals are likely to vote for different political parties from one election to the next invites further theory building and in-depth analysis on why swing voters behave the way they do (Hare and Kutsuris 2022). In Section 4.1.2, we will discuss how prediction can help inform inferential social science, theory building, and exploring experimental data – and help do so in a reproducible manner.

4.1.2 The Bias-Variance Tradeoff

Machine learning is primarily concerned with identifying relationships in observed data that will generalize to new, unobserved data. Importantly, the $\hat{f}(x)$ that best represents Y in our observed data will be at least slightly different from the true $f(x)$. This is another way of saying that while we want to use $\hat{f}(x)$ to learn about the underlying data generating process from the data we observe, we don't want to learn too much from the data we observe, as this may result in bad predictions for new data. In order to make more generalizable predictions – that is, to reduce our model's *variance* – we are willing to tolerate some *bias*. This *bias-variance tradeoff* is central to machine learning.

Bias refers to systematic (i.e., nonrandom) deviations from the underlying data generating process. Social life is incredibly complex: We can never expect to estimate a model that maps onto the true data generating process perfectly. We necessarily have to simplify the truth when building statistical models (or scientific theories). This creates bias.

Variance refers to how different of an answer we would have gotten if we had trained the same model on different data. We most often have just one set of data on which to train our model, but there is an arbitrarily large number of other datasets we could have collected. Variance refers to any fluctuations we would see by fitting the same model to these other training data.

As a general rule, bias and variance are negatively correlated. As we decrease the bias, we increase the variance (and vice versa). Our best approximation of $f(x)$ will be in the "sweet spot" that balances the two (often done by cross-validation, described in Section 4.1.3).

To demonstrate, we specify a data generating process, $f(x)$, that we have full control over. This function represents the nature of the relationship between two variables with random noise: $Y = 2x + x^2 + \epsilon$. We then simulate two datasets from this function, each with fifty observations. In Figure 1, the first row are three different models fit to the first dataset; the second row fits the same models to the second dataset.

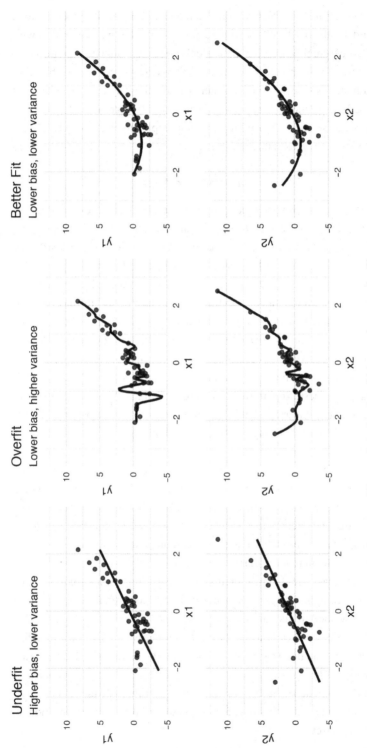

Figure 1 A simulated bias-variance tradeoff

The first model (left column) is a simple linear regression with no quadratic term. We see that it barely changes from one dataset to the next (low variance), but it does not fit the curve of the data very well (high bias). This is referred to as "underfitting," as we are learning less from the data than we could. The second column is local regression with a very narrow span, which means that it's fitting many regression lines on narrow windows along the x-axis, and then smoothing them out. We can see that it fits the data very closely (low bias), but it also changes a lot from the first dataset to the second (high variance). This is called "overfitting," as we are picking up too much information that is specific to the sample data we observe. The third column is a local regression line with a wider span. We see it fits the data reasonably well, without changing too much from dataset to dataset.

One way we can introduce some bias to decrease variance – and prevent overfitting – is through *smoothing* our estimated $\hat{f}(x)$. The lines in the right-most column of Figure 1 are much smoother than in the middle column. There are a variety of ways to smooth models as a way of preventing overfitting. We will discuss a few options as they relate to specific models in later sections.

4.1.3 Held-Out Data and Cross-Validation

Recall that the primary objective of supervised machine learning is to generate useful predictions on unseen data. We estimate a model from inputs X_1 and outputs Y_1, with the subscript denoting it is from the first dataset. We then apply this model to new data (let's call it the second dataset), where we know the inputs X_2 but *not* the outputs. We use the model trained on dataset 1 to estimate $\hat{Y}_2$. (Note the ^ on top to indicate that we are estimating this outcome – we haven't actually observed it.)

This makes sense in industry settings, where we train models that are then put into production to predict, for example, if a credit card charge is fraudulent, if a song should be recommended to a user, or how well a movie coming out next month will do in the box office. There is not a great analogue to basic social science research. Studies take precious time, labor, and money to run. It is typically not feasible to run a smaller version of the same study again purely as a means to validate a machine learning model.

Moreover, we cannot just fit the model to our data and validate it on the same data. How will we know if the model is overfitting those specific data? How do we know if it generalizes? One common option is to create a *held-out* set. This is also commonly referred to as making *training* and *testing* data. The idea is to randomly select, for example, 75 percent of our data to be used in fitting the model. The remaining 25 percent will be excluded, or held out, from estimation.

This 25 percent will then serve as our unseen data that we can use to validate our model by predicting outcomes in this held-out set and evaluating how useful those predictions are (however we have defined "useful," such as accuracy or sensitivity).

Another issue arises in model estimation, however, which is that (as shown in Figure 1) there are many different ways to "smooth" $\hat{f}(x)$. Machine learning models give researchers control over this using *hyperparameters*, or parameters that cannot be estimated from the data. This differentiates them from standard parameters, like regression coefficients, which refer to aspects of the data themselves. The researcher must make decisions regarding these hyperparameters. How much soothing should we impose on our model? Should we include an interaction term? Should we include a polynomial term? Or many polynomials? And so on.

We want to make these decisions on, again, unseen data to prevent overfitting. But we've already held out 25 percent of our data. What do we do with the other 75 percent? We can do something similar, called *cross-validation*. This is often referred to as *k*-fold cross-validation, since we cut up our training data into *k* folds (i.e., chunks), estimate the data on all but one chunk, validate on this held-out chunk, and repeat for all *k* folds (Figure 2). We then average performance across all folds.

For a concrete example, imagine we have a dataset of N = 10,000 observations. We want to test if there should be a polynomial term in the model or not. Specifically, this means testing whether $\hat{Y} = \beta_0 + \beta_1 X + \beta_2 X^2$ is better at predicting the outcome than $\hat{Y} = \beta_0 + \beta_1 X$. In other contexts, we might want to make other comparisons, such as whether different variables, models, or processing decisions (such as the inclusion of interaction terms) improve predictive performance.

We begin by randomly partitioning our 10,000 observations into two subsets: a "training" set that includes 75 percent (7,500) of our observations and a "test" set that includes the remaining 25 percent (2,500). The test set is held out until

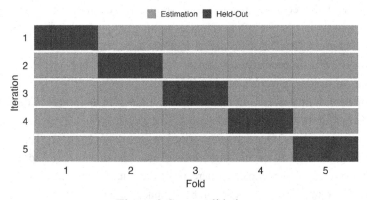

Figure 2 Cross-validation

after our models have been trained. The training data are then further partitioned into "folds" that we will use for in-sample cross-validation. Here, we use five folds, though it is common to use more (ten is the default in many statistical packages). Indeed, each "fold" can be a single observation such that the number of folds, k, is equal to the number of observations, n. This is often referred to as leave-one-out cross-validation.

Each of the folds in Figure 2 contains 1,500 data points (since 7,500 rows / 5 folds = 1,500). We will perform five iterations for each of the candidate models (with and without the X^2 term). On the first iteration, data from folds two through five will be used to estimate the model. Then we will test the models on fold one. Next, data from folds one and three through five are used for estimating the model; it is then tested on fold two – and so on, through the fifth iteration. It is important to clarify that because a given observation is used for both training and validation at different times, cross-validation should not be considered a substitute for constructing a separate held-out set to evaluate model performance (Bates, Hastie, and Tibshirani 2021).

For example, let's say we are using mean squared error (MSE) to compare the models: For each held-out fold, we calculate the MSE by averaging the squared distances between predicted and observed outcomes. We then average across all the folds for each model to determine the cross-validation MSE, selecting the model with the lowest such metric. However, to actually evaluate that model, we refit it using all of the training data (i.e., all five folds) and estimate the final MSE using the held-out data – that 25 percent we set aside at the beginning, which was never used to supervise the relationship between our independent and dependent variables.

The logic here is that we are always evaluating our models using data that they did not "see" when we estimated them. This helps us avoid overfitting. We can then have more confidence that the model will generalize to other unseen data and that relationships we observe are not just due to idiosyncrasies in our specific dataset.

4.2 Example Methods

While a full rundown of all common machine learning methods is beyond the scope of the Element, here we introduce two specific methods that will help inform subsequent sections.

4.2.1 Penalized Regression

Ordinary least squares (OLS) regression is named as such because it finds a solution for the coefficients that minimizes the sum of squared residuals (also known as the residual sum of squares, or RSS): If each person in our data is represented by i, we want to find the coefficients that minimize the sum of $(y_i - \hat{y}_i)^2$ across all N individuals in our data. In this equation, y_i represents the value we observe for the dependent variable of individual i, and $\hat{y}_i$ refers to their predicted value from the OLS equation. The predicted value is given by $\hat{y}_i = \beta_0 + \beta_1 x_{i1} + \beta_2 x_{i2} + \ldots + \beta_p x_{ip}$, where there are p predictors in our dataset.

Under standard assumptions, OLS minimizes the residual sum of squared errors without biasing estimates in any particular direction, which is why it is referred to as the "best linear unbiased estimator" (BLUE). Note the word "unbiased" and recall the tradeoff between bias and variance. In a machine learning context, we are willing to introduce some bias in order to lower variance. We can do that through penalized regression using a process known as *shrinkage* or *regularization*.

Penalized regression can be thought of as an extension of OLS.[2] Instead of minimizing RSS alone, it tries to minimize the RSS plus a *shrinkage* penalty. This penalty can be based on the coefficients' absolute values, producing least absolute shrinkage selection operator (LASSO) regression; the sum of squared coefficient values, which is referred to as "ridge" regression; or a weighted average of the two, referred to as the "elastic net." Here, we focus on the LASSO, the penalty for which is represented by $\lambda \sum_{j=1}^{p} |\beta_j|$.

In words, this LASSO penalty takes the absolute value of each of the p coefficients, adds them all up, and multiples them by a *hyperparameter* called λ. This product is then added to the loss function, such that the solution to the LASSO regression produces coefficients that minimize the residual sum of squared errors *plus* this penalty on the coefficients' absolute values. This means that when λ is zero, there is no penalty and we are left with traditional regression. As λ increases, we are placing higher penalties on model complexity and encouraging more coefficients to be discarded, or "shrink" to zero.

This LASSO penalty explicitly introduces bias into our model – our estimate of $\hat{f}(x)$ is no longer BLUE as it would be under OLS – but this bias will come with a reduction in variance.[3] The task then becomes selecting the optimal λ that balances the tradeoff between the two. We typically do so by using cross-validation, trying a range of λ values and settling on the one that

---

[2] Penalized regression can also be extended to other forms of generalized linear models, such as logistic regression for binary outcomes.

[3] Blackwell and Olson (2022b) introduce methods to reduce this form of *direct regularization bias* when using LASSO-based approaches to estimate effect heterogeneity. Their methods are also designed to reduce *indirect regularization bias* that emerges when models designed to predict outcomes are used to characterize heterogeneity in the relationship between a specific variable, such as an experimental treatment, and an outcome.

Table 4 OLS and LASSO results, simulated data

Term	LASSO Coefficient	OLS Coefficient	OLS Standard Error	OLS *t*-value	OLS *p*-value
(Intercept)	2.00	2.01	0.04	45.13	0.00
X1	2.91	3.08	0.04	70.02	0.00
X2	3.88	4.05	0.04	94.44	0.00
X3	0.00	0.00	0.04	0.11	0.92
X4	0.00	0.03	0.04	0.79	0.43
X5	0.00	0.03	0.04	0.62	0.54
X6	0.00	−0.03	0.04	−0.69	0.49
X7	0.00	0.03	0.04	0.74	0.46
X8	0.00	0.08	0.04	1.79	0.07
X9	0.00	−0.01	0.04	−0.20	0.84
X10	0.00	0.13	0.04	2.92	0.00

produces the lowest cross-validation error. This penalty is sensitive to the scale of each independent variable, so we always put each of our predictor variables on a common scale (such as *z-scoring* them by subtracting their mean and dividing by their standard deviation) before implementing LASSO regression.

Consider a simple example: We have observed an outcome and ten independent variables we think may predict the outcome. For simplicity's sake, let's say that the outcome is only in fact influenced by two of these, following the equation: $Y = 2 + 3X_1 + 4X_2 + \epsilon$, where each of the ten X_j variables and the error term follow a standard normal distribution with a mean of 0 and standard deviation of 1. We simulate 500 data points from this equation and fit both an OLS and LASSO regression model. The results are shown in Table 4.

While these estimates are broadly similar, we note two key differences. The first key difference concerns the terms we know are actually associated with the outcome (the intercept, X1, and X2). The OLS estimates for these variables are very close to their true values of 2, 3, and 4, respectively, while in the LASSO the coefficients for X1 and X2 are (by design) biased slightly toward zero. The second key difference concerns the latter eight *X* variables. In the OLS model, they tend to be close to zero, but two coefficients (for X8 and X10) still achieve low *p*-values. If we didn't know in advance (because we manually specified the data generating process) that these associations were the product of random chance, we might think that one or both of these variables carried a meaningful relationship with the outcome. In the LASSO, the coefficients corresponding with variables we know are unrelated to the outcome are *exactly* zero. They have been completely discarded by the model (λ selected by cross-validation was 0.17).

So, which model performs better on unseen data? We simulate another 500 cases from the same equation, use the OLS and LASSO models fit with the first 500 cases to predict Y, and see which has a lower MSE, the mean $(y_i - \hat{y}_i)^2$ across all N data points. The MSE when predicting Y in unseen data using OLS is 0.99, while it is 0.95 for the LASSO. Even though it introduces some bias, we get a lower MSE on *unseen* data by shrinking coefficients toward (or all the way to) zero.

4.2.2 Classification and Regression Trees

Penalized regression models such as the LASSO are direct extensions of standard linear regression. These models are *parametric*, in that they generate sets of parameters (coefficients) associated with independent variables. These models are also *linear*, in that a unit change in an independent variable is always associated with a specific change in the dependent variable, as described by that independent variable's parameter.

However, this is not the only way to use a set of independent variables to predict an outcome. Supervised machine learning provides us with a set of companion, *tree-based* methods that are both nonparametric and nonlinear (Montgomery and Olivella 2018).

In its most basic formulation, a decision tree is an algorithm that recursively partitions, or "splits," the data along independent variables that explain variation in the outcome. By *recursive*, we mean that subsets of the data are repeatedly split into smaller subsets until the algorithm reaches its designated stopping rule. Here, we focus on classification and regression trees, or CART models. Whether a tree-based model is a classification or regression tree simply refers to whether the outcome of interest is categorical (classification) or numeric (regression). In keeping with the nature analogy, "branches," or splits, in a decision tree end at "leaves," or nodes.

Consider a simple example using a small set of variables from the 2020 American National Election Survey. The dendrogram plotted in Figure 3 shows how we might build a decision tree for this data seeking to sort respondents based on their partisan identification, measured on a scale from one to seven with "1" representing "Strong Democrat," "7" representing "Strong Republican," and "4" representing independents who do not lean toward either party. In the plot, darker colors correspond with higher average scores on this measure of partisanship. For simplicity, we'll only partition groups of at least ten respondents – our designated stopping rule – and consider a relatively small

Simple Decision Tree: Partisan Identification

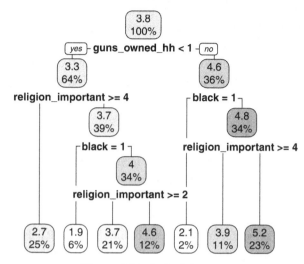

Figure 3 Basic decision tree

set of covariates. Specifically, we'll consider respondents' race, sex, education (whether they've completed a four-year degree), age, household income, importance of religion to their life, number of guns owned in the household, and geographic identity (whether the respondent considers themselves more of an urban or rural person).

The results are shown in Figure 3. At the top, before we partition the data, we see that the average partisan identification for all respondents is 3.8 on the 1–7 scale. We then split the data by gun ownership: 64 percent of our respondents live in households without guns, and their average partisan identification is 3.3; the 36 percent of respondents with at least one gun in the household are more Republican, averaging 4.6. Next, the group that does not own guns is split by whether they consider religion "very" or "extremely" important to their life, while the gun-owning group is split by race (specifically, whether respondents identify as Black or African American). These variables are then used again on the other side of the tree, respectively, for further splits. The other variables we consider, such as age or income, are less useful for separating Democrats from Republicans once gun ownership, race, and the importance of religion to the respondent's life have been taken into account (bearing in mind, of course, that this is a heavily simplified example).

Different tree-based models will apply different decision rules for determining which splits to make for which variables at each level of the tree. As with penalized regression models, tree-based models also have hyperparameters that the researcher can specify: defining how deep the tree(s) should go or, depending on the type of tree-based model, how many iterations of the algorithm to run, and so on. The previous decision to prevent partitions of groups with fewer than ten survey respondents was one such example. More shallow trees (i.e., CART models that make fewer splits) will have higher bias but lower variance. Deeper tree depth – that is, making more splits – will tend to lower bias but raise variance.

4.2.2.1 Ensemble Regularization

Classification and regression trees (CART models) offer different strategies to avoid overfitting than their parametric counterparts. These tend to fall under the general family of *ensemble* methods, which generate high performance by aggregating predictions from multiple models that would be less accurate on their own. While ensemble methods are not limited to CART models, CART models tend to incorporate some form of ensemble regularization. It is also important to keep in mind that, as with penalized regression, ensemble regularization is a means to an end: reducing the variance in our models to improve their out-of-sample performance.

There are three main types of ensemble methods: bagging, boosting, and stacking. We provide a brief overview of each here.

Bagging, short for "bootstrapped aggregation," involves fitting the same model on bootstrapped resamples of the data (i.e., resampling with replacement) and letting each version of the model "vote" on the prediction task (Breiman 1996). As the model is refit to each bootstrapped resample, the trees grown in a bagged CART model are loosely correlated in that each tree is only learning from its own resample of the data, not from the other trees. For continuous outcomes, predictions are then generated by averaging those from all models; for classification tasks, predictions are decided by plurality vote. The widely used random forest algorithm (Breiman 2001) is a bagged learner that extends this method by also randomly sampling which independent variables to consider when fitting each tree (with, you guessed it, a hyperparameter determining how many variables are randomly selected at a time).

Boosting involves sequentially fine-tuning a model by giving more weight to observations that generated higher prediction errors in previous iterations (Friedman 2002). Unlike bagged models, the trees fit in a boosted CART model are *dependent* on each other. After one tree is fit, the next considers information from that previous tree: The observations that were harder to predict are given more weight. Put simply, boosted models attempt to learn from their mistakes. This can make them more computationally expensive than bagged models but also potentially more powerful. AdaBoost (Freund and Schapire 1996) and XGBoost (Chen and Guestrin 2016) are two of the more popular algorithms for fitting boosted CART models. Among other hyperparameters specific to each, both require the researcher to set a hyperparameter for the number of rounds to refit the model. More rounds will tend to reduce bias and increase variance.

Stacking involves fitting multiple different *types* of models to build a meta-learner. The meta-learner's predictions are constructed by taking the weighted average of predictions from each of the base models, with weights based on each base model's performance relative to the other models in the ensemble. Political scientists have used stacked models to model complex phenomena like swing voting (Hare and Kutsuris 2022) and to estimate heterogeneous treatment effects in experiments (Grimmer, Messing, and Westwood 2017), which we will discuss in later sections. Stacked models are arbitrarily complex, as they involve selecting which (and how many) base models to estimate as well as the hyperparameters for those models. For example, a researcher could build a "stacked" meta-learner out of all of the previous learners we have just discussed, combining information from a penalized regression, bagged CART model, and boosted CART model. For this reason, we do not cover them in depth here, though we recommend the **SuperLearner** package in R if you would like to explore them on your own (Polley et al. 2021).

4.2.2.2 CART Models in Practice

Recall the example from Section 4.2.1, which we used to demonstrate penalized regression: We have 500 simulated observations with 10 independent variables that are all normally distributed with a mean of 0 and a standard deviation of 1. The true data generating process is represented by $Y = 2 + 3X_1 + 4X_2 + \epsilon$, and the remaining 8 independent variables are pure noise. Here, we'll use that same data to demonstrate CART models.

We randomly partition these data into a training set of 350 observations and a test set of the remaining 150. We then fit six models to the training data and use them to predict outcomes in the test data, storing the MSE for each set of out-of-sample predictions. The first three of these models are single decision trees with different hyperparameter specifications. One uses the **tree** package's (Ripley 2021) defaults: a minimum node size of 10 (meaning that the tree will stop growing if any leaf holds fewer than 10 observations) and a minimum within-node deviance of 0.01 (which governs whether there is enough variation in the outcome within a given node to split it). The second model increases the complexity by both allowing for deeper tree depth and lowering the minimum within-node deviance, while the third model is fully saturated (minimum node size = 2; minimum deviance = 0), meaning we will grow the tree as deep as we can. The next three models are our ensemble learners: the first is a random forest with default hyperparameter settings (Wright and Ziegler 2017); the next two use XGBoost for either two or five rounds of boosting, respectively (Chen et al. 2022).

Results from this procedure are plotted in Figure 4, with separate facets for each model. The true outcome in the test set is represented on the x-axis, with corresponding predictions on the y-axis. The dashed lines represent perfect fit; the solid lines represent the line of best fit between observations and predictions. The MSE for each model is labeled within the facet.

The results provide an additional demonstration of the bias-variance tradeoff. On the one hand, the simple decision trees tend to be less biased than the ensemble models, with lines of best fit between prediction and outcome hewing closer to the line of perfect fit. The slopes of the relationships between observations and predictions in the ensemble models are less than one, indicating that these models are (to varying degrees) biased toward zero – as were the penalized regression models from earlier in this section. However, this introduction of bias can buy us substantial reductions in variance. The five-round XGBoost model outperforms all of the simpler decision trees with respect to MSE; the default random forest outperforms the default and saturated decision trees. The XGBoost model with only two rounds of training performs much worse and is much more biased, highlighting the importance of paying attention to the hyperparameters you use when deploying these models and testing how decisions you make with respect to hyperparameter selection affect your model's performance on unseen data.

4.3 Machine Learning Is Exploratory and Reproducible

This section introduced concepts and methods that distinguish supervised machine learning from classical statistics, such as the bias-variance tradeoff, held-out validation, and regularization. It then demonstrated how these concepts and methods are useful for systematically identifying patterns in observed data that generalize to new, unobserved data. Put another way, it demonstrated how machine learning is both exploratory and reproducible in nature.

These methods are exploratory in that they require minimal to no theoretical expectations. This does not mean that these methods take away all human decision-making. As the researcher, you are still responsible for deciding

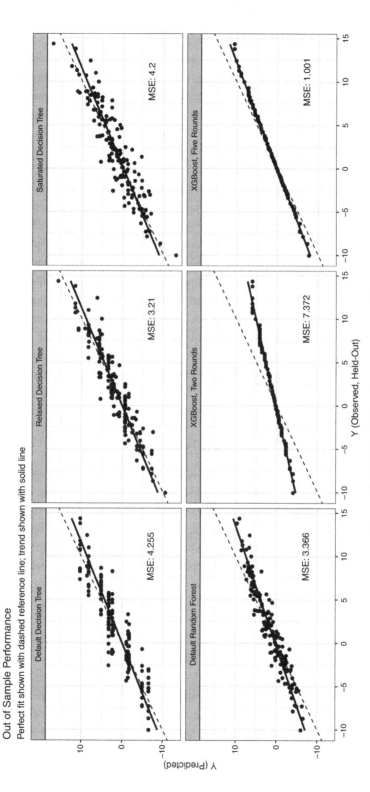

Figure 4 CART model performance comparison

which variables to consider, how those variables will be preprocessed, how to tune your hyperparameters, and so on. But if, for example, you decide to consider interactions between variables, you are not responsible for deciding which interactions to test. Machine learning methods allow you to systematically explore the full scope of potential interactions. This is especially useful if and when there are nonlinear relationships lurking in your data that you have not anticipated (Beiser-McGrath and Beiser-McGrath 2020).

These methods are reproducible in that machine learning models are evaluated based on their performance on data not used to train the models themselves. That is, a machine learning workflow will include both an exploratory (training) and confirmatory (testing) stage in a single analysis. This is essential for guarding against overfitting, which we would surely do if we, for example, fit a single OLS regression that included every possible interaction term. That said, these methods do not guarantee that your findings will replicate in a completely new study, nor does using a particular method establish that your research is fully reproducible. The decisions you make before you run your model can still send you down a particular road in the garden of forking paths. However, these methods are useful as a tool for conducting analyses that are exploratory in nature in a principled, reproducible manner. This will be especially important for the purposes of using machine learning to characterize treatment effect heterogeneity, which we take up in the next section.

5 Bringing It Together

We have reviewed the core principles and intuitions behind causal inference and machine learning separately. We hope that we provided an understanding of the potential outcomes framework for causal inference, the distinctions between the goals inference and the goals of prediction, and how machine learning models navigate the bias-variance tradeoff to make useful predictions.

We reviewed these methodological approaches separately in part because they developed separately. However, the core argument of this Element is that strict boundaries between the two are unnecessary. As we noted in Section 2, causal claims often double as predictions. To say that X causes Y is to predict that changing the value of X will change the value of Y. To say that a study failed to replicate is to say that the relationships it identified were not robust to out-of-sample prediction.

As such, it is becoming increasingly common to apply the core principles and methodological approaches from machine learning to research questions concerning causal mechanisms. Rather than using machine learning to make useful predictions of an outcome of interest, researchers instead use machine learning to make useful predictions of a given treatment's effect on an outcome of interest. This approach is particularly useful for systematically recovering treatment effect heterogeneity (i.e., moderating variables), to which we now turn.

5.1 Varying Treatment Effects

The first analysis many social scientists do after running an experiment is a regression or t-test that estimates the effect some treatment had on an outcome variable. Researchers might also add relevant covariates to the regression model to protect against any violations of random assignment along important variables. Either way, this involves estimating the expected value of the dependent variable (e.g., mean for OLS, probability for the logistic model) in each experimental condition. The causal effects are the differences between these conditions. As discussed in Section 2, this is known as the "average treatment effect" in the potential outcomes framework (Rubin 1974; Holland 1986).

The average treatment effect is so named because, due to the fundamental problem of causal inference, we cannot observe the treatment effect for each individual (remembering that we observe each respondent in only one of the experimental conditions). So, using the aforementioned statistical methods, we calculate the average difference between treated and untreated outcomes across all participants and use this as our estimate of the effect we expect that treatment to have for everyone.

While this is useful information, it is often unsatisfying. In practice, it is unrealistic to assume that the average treatment effect applies equally to every observation. All treatment effects vary to a certain extent, and we waste precious data when we do not even attempt to explore this variation (Campbell 1973; Cronbach 1975; Gelman 2015). To put it in terms of regression, treatment effect variation refers to "interaction terms" or "moderating variables": The treatment effect depends on the value of some other variable (whether observed or unobserved).

It may seem like a radical statement to say that *all* treatment effects vary, but this is mostly due to how difficult it is to quantify this variation. Often, treatment effect variation is too small to be of substantive interest, to say nothing of being statistically detectable. But even when we have strong reasons to suspect our treatment effects to vary, it is often difficult to quantitatively distinguish conditional average treatment effects from average treatment effects. Interactions require large samples or effect sizes to achieve the requisite power to observe them using linear models (McClelland and Judd 1993). When we cannot make these quantitative distinctions, the average treatment effect is left as our best estimate of the effect we can expect our treatment to have on any given unit.

But consider even some of the most replicated effects, such as the Stroop effect. Individuals are shown names of colors and asked to report the font color in which these names are printed. People respond more slowly when the colors are incongruent (when the word "yellow" is printed in blue, for example) than when they are congruent (when the word "yellow" is printed in yellow). This treatment effect varies: Incongruence delays response times for some more than others, and this variation can be systematically explained by demographic variables (Nicosia, Cohen-Shikora, and Balota 2021). In political science, researchers frequently find that the effects of partisan politicians' messaging vary by respondents' partisan or ideological identity (Nicholson 2012; Grimmer, Messing, and Westwood 2017). There is always variation in treatment effects. The question is the extent of this variation and whether we have enough data and observe the relevant moderating variables to quantify it.

This treatment effect variation is important for generalizability and replicability – a point that has been noted for at least half a century. Consider Cronbach (1975), who argued that any generalization of an effect from a laboratory experiment to the "real world" is necessarily changing the context in which the effect was first found. This generalization introduces what we might now call "hidden moderators." Cronbach urged experimental social scientists to "reflect on what it means to establish empirical generalizations in a world in which most effects are interactive" (p. 121). Decades later, a failure to account for effect heterogeneity continues to threaten the external validity of experimental findings (Bryan, Tipton, and Yeager 2021).

Both Campbell (1973) and Gelman (2015) make similar observations. These authors argue that social science is more variable than physical sciences. We have fewer "laws of nature," since the social world changes more quickly than the natural world. Thus, it is particularly important for experimental social scientists to explore interactions in their data. Questions such as "did this study replicate or did it not replicate?" present a false dichotomy analogous to questions such as "is there an effect or isn't there?" Gelman (2015) argues that assuming constant effect sizes "corresponds to a simplified view of the world that can impede research discussion" and that allowing for interactions lets us engage "with the world's complexity" (p. 363).

In the second part of this Element, we introduce machine learning-based methods for analyzing experimental data. These tools are especially useful for systematically exploring such data to identify treatment effect variation, or "heterogeneous treatment effects," in ways that are more likely to generalize to new data than searching for moderators using OLS and fishing for significant p-values. These methods are exploratory in nature, but they are principled. They offer a different solution than pre-registration for a similar problem: an individual researcher running a multitude of linear regressions with different sets of specified interaction effects in an unprincipled, disorganized fashion. The methods presented in the next few sections aim to explore the data for interactions – but they do so following algorithmic procedures designed to guard against overfitting the data (i.e., finding illusory interactions).

We begin with prediction rule ensembles. Prediction rule ensembles involve fitting shallow boosted decision trees, deriving rules based on the splits in these trees, and fitting a LASSO regression with those rules as independent variables to discard those that are trivial or redundant. A researcher can then examine which (if any) of these rules that are useful for predicting the outcome contain the experimental condition and which (if any) other covariates these rules include. Crucially for experimental social scientists, prediction rule ensembles place a particular emphasis on interpretability. By strictly limiting tree depth, the resulting rules are easy to understand and communicate.

We then discuss the causal random forest. This method builds on the traditional random forest by determining splits in the data based on differences in conditional average treatment effects rather than differences in the outcome itself. Importantly, the causal random forest estimates splits in each tree using one half of the data and predicts the treatment effects using the other half, building the principles of held-out estimation into its algorithm. Not only does this guard against overfitting; it also allows researchers to calculate confidence intervals around treatment effect estimates at the level of the individual respondent.

The two methods we demonstrate here are by no means exhaustive. Recent years have seen a variety of machine learning–based approaches for estimating heterogeneous treatment effects in social scientific research (Imai and Strauss 2011; Green and Kern 2012; Imai and Ratkovic 2013; Grimmer, Messing, and Westwood 2017; Ratkovic and Tingley 2017; Künzel et al. 2019; Blackwell and Olson 2022b; Ham, Imai, and Janson 2022). These methods differ in their specifics, but all borrow from the core principles we have discussed in this and previous sections. Our goal is not only for you to be able to use the R code from the upcoming sections in your own work but also to understand how and why these methods work. That way, you will be able to understand and familiarize yourself with other approaches for using machine learning to analyze experiments, including new ones as they are inevitably introduced in this rapidly developing field.

6 Prediction Rule Ensembles

The prediction rule ensemble (PRE) is a method that combines two machine learning approaches to identify interpretable, robust relationships within sample data. It works in two steps. First, it fits shallow boosted regression trees. Second, it uses the terminal nodes from these decision trees to form indicator independent variables (or "rules") in a penalized regression (typically a LASSO) to determine the parameters in the final model (Fokkema 2020; Fokkema and Strobl 2020).

Prediction rule ensembles are particularly well-suited for experimental social science because they balance the benefits of tree-based ensemble methods (predictive accuracy, nonlinear relationships) with the interpretability of linear regression. The final ensemble will produce a table of rules that closely resembles that of a regression coefficient table. This interpretability may sacrifice some accuracy, but you as a researcher may be willing to make this trade for the purposes of theory building and hypothesis testing. Finally, while we demonstrate prediction rule ensembles for experimental data here, we note that the method is useful for identifying interaction effects that are both likely to generalize to unseen data and easy to interpret and communicate in other contexts as well.

6.1 How Prediction Rule Ensembles Work

We describe prediction rule ensembles conceptually here and provide a tutorial. For a detailed look at the mathematical details behind the method, we recommend Fokkema and Strobl (2020). And while we mostly stick to the default settings here, we recommend also reading Fokkema (2020) for a detailed look at what the software is capable of.

Prediction rule ensembles are fit in two steps: rule generation and rule selection. We describe each in turn.

6.1.1 Rule Generation

In Section 4, we discussed classification and regression trees. These involve recursively splitting the data along values of the independent variables in a way that best explains variation in the dependent variable. We can conceptualize each of these branches as a "rule," on which individuals either score 1 (yes) or 0 (no). For example, consider a hypothetical decision tree predicting support for the Black Lives Matter movement among White and Black respondents only. We use race and political identification as predictors. Imagine the decision tree first makes a partition at race: For Black respondents, the mean level of support is 6.2 on a 7-point scale. Then, it makes a partition for White respondents by political identification: For White Democrats, mean support is 5.3 – while the mean support is 2.7 for White Republicans. These three terminal nodes of the tree – Black respondents, White Democrats, and White Republicans – can be formulated into categorical variables, or "rules," where a respondent either meets that rule (1) or doesn't (0).

We can then write down these rules as a regression equation. Let X refer to the first partition, whether the respondent is Black (1) or not (0). Then, let W refer to if the respondent is a White Democrat, while Z indicates if the respondent is a White Republican. The regression equation is then: $\hat{y} = 6.2(X) + 5.3(W) + 2.7(Z)$. We could also move X to the intercept and simplify as: $\hat{y} = 6.2 - 0.9(W) - 2.5(Z)$. This is the first step in generating a PRE, although it does it hundreds of times and uses boosting.

By default, a PRE will start by creating 500 decision trees, each using a random subsample of half of the data and each having a maximum depth of 3. This maximum depth means that rules will involve no more than three variables, and so the most complicated relationships we could potentially identify are three-way interactions. This keeps the model interpretable. As these trees are boosted (discussed in Section 4), each tree is fit sequentially. Cases with greater prediction errors in previous trees are given more weight in subsequent trees.[4] Of course, one can change these hyperparameters. You can fit more or fewer decision trees, with higher or lower maximum depth, with different learning rates when boosting. You can also vary which specific decision tree algorithm to use or if you would prefer the decision trees to be bagged rather than boosted.

Each terminal node from every tree is turned into a binary rule, like the aforementioned example, and these rules are defined as variables for use in subsequent regression: A specific case is coded 1 if it meets that rule (i.e., if it is in that terminal node in that tree) and 0 otherwise. Confirmatory rules can also be specified beforehand; for example, an experimental condition can be forced to be included and unpenalized. This could help in model comparison by seeing if our hypothesized confirmatory rules improve performance. By default, prediction rule ensembles also include linear terms for every variable without interactions.

6.1.2 Rule Selection

This procedure produces a regression equation with hundreds of predictor variables. Using OLS in this context would produce results that suffer from multicollinearity, may not be identified, are overfit to the training data, and are uninterpretable. Prediction rule ensembles address these issues in two ways.

---

[4] Even though we use a random subsample of observations to fit a tree, that tree can generate predictions (and prediction errors) for all observations when determining which cases should be given more weight for the next tree.

First, the algorithm drops rules that are perfectly collinear (i.e., duplicate terms or perfectly complementary terms). Then, linear terms are normalized to match the variance of rules and a LASSO penalty is added to the model. The λ value – how strictly to penalize coefficients – is determined by ten fold cross-validation. Again, prediction rule ensembles are very versatile: Linear terms can be excluded or included, one could use a ridge or elastic net constraint instead of a LASSO, and the cross-validation procedure for selecting λ could be changed.

This results in a sparse model limited to rules that were not shrunk to zero by the LASSO regression. Each rule is a binary variable that either adds to or subtracts from the respondent's score on the outcome. Prediction rule ensembles can also be fit using a binary outcome variable, where each rule would add to or subtract from that case's score on the logit scale. We turn to a worked example to show how prediction rule ensembles could be used in experimental social science, particularly in helping find variables that interact with the treatment.

6.2 A Worked Example

We demonstrate the prediction rule ensemble here using an experiment among likely Democratic presidential primary voters fielded in June 2019 by YouGov on behalf of Data for Progress, a left-leaning think tank.[5] The experiment employed a conjoint design to study which attributes likely Democratic primary voters valued in prospective candidates for president in 2020. Respondents were shown profiles for two hypothetical candidates, Candidate A and Candidate B, who were each given a randomly generated race, gender, age, climate plan, health care plan, general election strategy, and background with respect to their relationship to the Washington "establishment."

There are a few reasons why we chose to use this dataset for our demonstration. The first is that the raw data are publicly available.[6] Another reason is that these data have been used elsewhere to address substantive and methodological research questions. See Green, Schaffner, and Luks (2023) for an example of these data being analyzed using traditional methods for conjoint experiments and Abramson et al. (2020) for an example of these data being analyzed with machine learning methods in greater detail.

Those examples leverage the full dataset, featuring nearly 3,000 respondents who each indicated their preferences in five matchups between hypothetical candidates. The core advantage of a conjoint design is that it allows us to estimate the marginal effects of particular attributes in situations – such as candidate

---

[5] At the time this survey was fielded, one of us, Mark, worked at YouGov; the other, Jon, was a cofounder of Data for Progress.

[6] You can find the data and codebook at: www.filesforprogress.org/datasets/pre_post_debate/.

evaluation – where many attributes are likely to matter. However, for the purposes of this demonstration, we want to treat this dataset as a more traditional experiment, and we want to estimate the effects of one specific attribute: candidate gender. We therefore subset these data to the following observations:

- The first pair of candidates the respondent chose between
- Matchups that featured a man versus a woman
- No missingness on any covariates we consider as potential moderators.

This leaves us with 1,384 observations where we can estimate whether – or perhaps *which* – Democratic primary voters preferred male or female candidates for the presidency.

6.2.1 Code

For space and efficiency, the code we walk through here picks up the analysis after the data (the "df" object below) have been cleaned and preprocessed for our analysis. Full replication materials, including this cleaning and preprocessing code, are included in the supplementary materials.

We begin our analysis by partitioning our data into training and testing sets. As discussed in earlier sections, we will use the smaller testing set to evaluate model performance.

```
# Packages this code uses
library(tidyverse)
library(pre)
library(MLmetrics)
library(knitr)
library(kableExtra)

# Always set a seed to make sure your analysis replicates!
set.seed(1839)

# Identify cases to be used for training and testing
  # Training cases: random sample of 75% of observations in df
cases <- sample(1:nrow(df), round(nrow(df) * .75))

# Training data: rows in training indices
dat_train <- df[cases, ]

# Test / held-out data: rows not in training indices
dat_test <- df[-cases, ]
```

We will evaluate four models.

The first model we will try is the default PRE, using the **pre** package (Fokkema 2020). This version simply applies the algorithm to best predict our outcome, a binary indicator of whether the respondent picked Candidate A over Candidate B, as a function of all of our covariates. These covariates include our experimental treatment of whether Candidate A or B is the male or female candidate, but here it is not treated any differently from other covariates, such as whether the respondent is a man or a woman.

We will call this our Default model.

```
set.seed(1839)

# Fit Model 1:
m1 <- pre(

    # Formula: picked Candidate A as a function of all covariates
    picked_cand_a ~ .,

    # Data: training set
    dat_train,

    # Since our outcome is binary, we specify a binomial model
    family = binomial,

    # Optional argument to print intermediate messages to the
    console
        # Set to TRUE in the replication materials
    verbose = FALSE
)
```

Our next model is similar to the first, except this time we will give our experimental treatment special consideration. That is, we will use the function's **confirmatory** argument to tell the algorithm to include this variable in the final ensemble, unpenalized. We do this because we are particularly interested, for theoretical reasons, in the effect of randomly varying which of Candidates A and B is a woman on the probability of the respondent preferring one over the other.

We will call this our Constrained model.

```
set.seed(1839)
m2 <- pre(
    picked_cand_a ~ .,
    dat_train,
    family = binomial,
    verbose = TRUE,

    # Manually include specific parameters using 'confirmatory'
        # These parameters will *not* be penalized
    confirmatory = 'cand_a_female %in% c("FALSE")'
)
```

Next, we model the outcome *without* considering our experimental treatment. We do this by simply removing our treatment variable from the data when calling the **pre()** function. This will provide us with a baseline estimate of how well we are able to predict our outcome of interest (picking Candidate A over Candidate B) without using information from our experiment. Given the randomization embedded into the rest of the data, we shouldn't observe much systematic variation in this outcome due to factors other than the treatment. If the previous two models outperform this one, it will tell us that the experimental treatment variable is useful for predicting the outcome.

We will call this our Naive model.

```
set.seed(1839)
m3 <- pre(
  picked_cand_a ~ .,

  # Remove treatment variable from training data for baseline
  comparison
  dplyr::select(dat_train, -cand_a_female),
  family = binomial,
  verbose = TRUE
)
```

Finally, we will consider modeling the outcome without considering any interactions between covariates. That is, we will specify a penalized regression analogous to a traditional logistic model, not using any of the prediction rules identified by our boosted regression trees. This baseline comparison will allow us to infer whether the additional complexity we introduce with our decision rules is useful for predicting the outcome.

We will call this our Linear model.

```
set.seed(1839)
m4 <- pre(
  picked_cand_a ~ .,
  dat_train,
  family = binomial,
  verbose = TRUE,

  # Specify type = "linear" for version without interactions
  type = "linear"
)
```

With our models trained, we then see how their predictions perform on the held-out training data.

We can start by defining accuracy as the rate at which our binary prediction for whether the respondent preferred Candidate A over Candidate B was correct and say that our best-fitting model is the one that maximizes this accuracy rate.

```
# Predict binary outcomes in test set
dat_test$m1_pred <- predict(m1, as.data.frame(dat_test), type =
"class")
dat_test$m2_pred <- predict(m2, as.data.frame(dat_test), type =
"class")
dat_test$m3_pred <- predict(m3, as.data.frame(dat_test), type =
"class")
dat_test$m4_pred <- predict(m4, as.data.frame(dat_test), type =
"class")

# Get accuracy for each set of predictions
    # For each binary prediction column in the test set
accuracies <- map_dbl(paste0("m", c(1:4), "_pred"), function(x)
{

    # Accuracy as the average of predictions equaling the outcome
    mean(dat_test$picked_cand_a == dat_test %>% pull(x))
})

# Make table, sort by accuracy
acc_table <- data.frame(
    Model = c("Default", "Constrained", "Naive", "Linear"),
    Accuracy = round(accuracies, 3)) %>%
    arrange(desc(Accuracy))

acc_table %>%
    arrange(desc(Accuracy)) %>%
    knitr::kable(format = "pipe",
                caption = "Model Comparison, Accuracy",
                label = "pre_accuracy")
```

As we can see, the Default model gives us the highest accuracy (Table 5), barely edging out the Constrained model (i.e., the one where we force the algorithm to consider, and not penalize, our treatment variable). Both of these models that use boosted classification trees are more accurate than both the Naive and the Linear models (the version that doesn't consider treatment assignment at all and the version that doesn't consider any interactions, respectively), which correctly classify the outcome at rates closer to chance.

Accuracy is an intuitive way to evaluate model performance in this context, especially since our outcome is relatively balanced (respondents pick Candidate

Table 5 Model comparison,
accuracy

Model	Accuracy
Default	0.590
Constrained	0.584
Linear	0.532
Naive	0.523

A about as often as they pick Candidate B), and we care just as much about Type I errors as Type II errors when predicting respondent preferences (i.e., predicting the respondent will prefer Candidate A when they don't is as bad as predicting the respondent won't prefer Candidate A when they do). But accuracy is not the only way to evaluate predictive performance and even in this context has limitations. For instance, judging by classification accuracy alone, a respondent who is predicted to have preferred Candidate A with a probability of 0.51 but actually preferred Candidate B is considered to be equally poorly classified as a respondent who is predicted to prefer Candidate A with probability 0.80 but actually preferred Candidate B. We might care about not only whether we miss but by how much.

Another way to put this is that accuracy might not be the appropriate *loss function*, or manner in which we quantify our predictions' deviations from their true outcomes, for evaluating our models' performance. There are many alternatives available. One such alternative is logarithmic loss.[7] Rather than considering binary classifications as one would with accuracy, the logarithmic loss compares observed outcomes (0s and 1s) to predicted probabilities (ranging between 0 and 1) and calculates a penalty based on the average of the natural log of the errors. This preserves more information about our models' predictions than simply whether they were correct or incorrect: Our models get more credit for more confident correct predictions and more blame for more confident incorrect predictions.

```
# Predict probability of binary outcome in test set
dat_test$m1_prob <- predict(m1, as.data.frame(dat_test), type =
"response")
dat_test$m2_prob <- predict(m2, as.data.frame(dat_test), type =
"response")
dat_test$m3_prob <- predict(m3, as.data.frame(dat_test), type =
"response")
dat_test$m4_prob <- predict(m4, as.data.frame(dat_test), type =
"response")
```

---

[7] In R, this can be calculated using the **LogLoss()** function in the **MLmetrics** package.

```
# Get logarithmic losses
  # For each probability column in the test set
losses <- map_dbl(paste0("m", c(1:4), "_prob"), function(x) {
  # Calculate logarithmic loss
  MLmetrics::LogLoss(
    y_pred = dat_test %>% pull(x),
    y_true = as.numeric(dat_test$picked_cand_a)
  )
})

# Make table, sort by logarithmic loss
loss_table <- data.frame(
    Model = c("Default", "Constrained", "Naive", "Linear"),
    LogLoss = round(losses, 3)) %>%
  arrange(LogLoss)

loss_table %>%
  arrange(LogLoss) %>%
  knitr::kable(format = "pipe",
               caption = "Model Comparison, Logarithmic Loss",
               label = "pre_logloss")
```

In this case, including the treatment variable and its interactions with other independent variables (in the Default and Constrained models) improves performance – whether performance is measured by accuracy (Table 5) or logarithmic loss (Table 6). The Constrained model slightly outperforms the Default model here, when evaluating using logarithmic loss, but the differences between the two based on either loss function are trivial. Similarly, the Naive model does slightly better than the Linear model in terms of logarithmic loss after ranking the worst as measured by overall accuracy, but these differences are very small and we do not want to risk overinterpreting them here.

Table 6 Model comparison, logarithmic loss

Model	LogLoss
Constrained	0.574
Default	0.581
Naive	0.604
Linear	0.614

Since the Constrained model narrowly outperforms the Default model as measured by log-loss, we will select it for further analysis (with the caveat that the differences between the two are minor). Now we want to interpret it. Prediction rule ensembles provide a few different ways of doing so.

First, we can examine which decision rules identified in this model have nonzero coefficients in our LASSO regression. These coefficients have interpretations analogous to traditional linear regression. Depending on whether the outcome is continuous or binary, they represent change in predicted outcome, or probability of observing a "success" in outcome (such as selecting Candidate A), conditional on the rule in question changing from 0 to 1. Unlike traditional regression, coefficients in penalized regression do not typically have parametric uncertainty estimates. That is, we do not calculate p-values for our decision rules to determine whether their relationship with our outcome is statistically distinguishable from zero. Here, a coefficient is statistically distinguished from zero if it is not zero after applying our LASSO penalty.

The coefficient table for our best-fitting model is shown in Table 7. Coefficients named for variables represent main effects. Coefficients named for rule numbers represent interactions reflected in decision rules, the contents of which are outlined in the "description" column. We present this table in a format analogous to what you would see in your R console; in your own work, you will want to rename rules and descriptions to be easier to communicate.

In this table, a few things stand out. At a basic level, our treatment variable (whether the hypothetical Candidate A is a man) has a negative coefficient. All else equal, we can infer that respondents were generally more likely to select Candidate A when Candidate A was a woman running against a man than when Candidate A was a man running against a woman. However, we also see that this variable is included in multiple other decision rules that carry nonzero coefficients. Which is to say, respondents with varying identities, attitudes, and backgrounds vary in the extent to which they preferred hypothetical women over men. For instance, the positive coefficient for Rule 23 indicates that preferences for women over men were stronger among respondents who both held a favorable opinion of the Democratic National Committee and said that warmth was a necessary trait for the eventual Democratic nominee to possess. The negative coefficient on Rule 3 indicates that respondents who identified as progressive were less likely to select Candidate A when that candidate ,was randomly presented as a man.

Table 7 PRE coefficients

rule	coefficient	description
cand_a_female %in% c ("FALSE")	−0.327	cand_a_female %in% c("FALSE")
(Intercept)	0.326	1
rule19	−0.221	region %in% c("Midwest", "West") & demnom %in% c("TRUE")
rule23	0.158	cand_a_female %in% c("TRUE") & candwarm %in% c("selected") & favdnc %in% c("TRUE")
rule2	0.117	cand_a_female %in% c("FALSE") & progressive %in% c("not selected")
urbanicityRural or other	−0.104	urbanicityRural or other
rule3	−0.096	cand_a_female %in% c("FALSE") & progressive %in% c("selected")
rule14	0.078	progressive %in% c("not selected") & urbanicity %in% c("Suburb")
considerwoman_n3	−0.036	considerwoman_n3
rule11	−0.019	horserace %in% c("Bernie", "Pete")
unfavwallstTRUE	−0.015	unfavwallstTRUE
rule6	0.001	urbanicity %in% c("City", "Suburb")

```
# Get coefficients from Model 2
coef(m2) %>%

    # Filter to non-zero coefficients
    filter(abs(coefficient) > 0) %>%

    # Sort descending by absolute value
    arrange(desc(abs(coefficient))) %>%

    # Format and print
    mutate(coefficient = round(coefficient, 3)) %>%
    knitr::kable(format = "pipe", caption = "PRE Coefficients",
              label = "pre_coefs")
```

Finally, we can examine which variables were most "important" in our model. Classification and regression tree models typically have some way of characterizing a metric called "variable importance," but this metric can be calculated in a variety of ways that may differ substantially from one model to the next. For example, variable importance can reflect how often a variable was

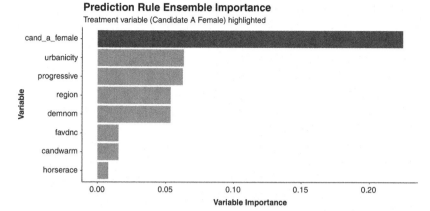

Figure 5 Variable importance

selected for partitioning the data, or how much predictive accuracy is lost when that variable is excluded from estimation. We generally view variable importance as a useful, *limited* heuristic for characterizing the nature of variation in one's data, and caution against heavily relying on or otherwise overinterpreting such measures.

In the context of prediction rule ensembles, variable importance is based on the absolute value of coefficients in which the given variable appears – either as a linear term or in a decision rule – after standardizing the coefficients to a common scale. Here, we see that our variable corresponding to our experimental treatment emerges as the most important variable for predicting our outcome (Figure 5). In a randomized conjoint experiment, this is to be expected. To the extent to which additional variables are useful for predicting our outcome in an experiment like this one, we should expect this to be due to their moderating effects on the treatment variable itself. Based on how importance is calculated here, their importance would also contribute to the treatment variable's importance.

```
# Get importance object
imp <- importance(m2)

# Plot
imp_plot <-
  imp$varimps %>%

  # Highlight treatment variable
  mutate(highlight = ifelse(grepl("female", varname),
1, .5)) %>%
```

```
ggplot(aes(x = fct_rev(fct_inorder(varname)),
           y = imp,
           alpha = factor(highlight)))+
scale_alpha_manual(name = "",
                   breaks = c(.5, 1),
                   values = c(.5, 1),
                   labels = c("other", "treatment"))+
guides(alpha = "none")+
geom_col()+
labs(x = "Variable", y = "Variable Importance",
     title = "Prediction Rule Ensemble Importance",
     subtitle = "Treatment variable (Candidate A Female)
     highlighted")+
coord_flip()+
theme_book()
```

6.3 Conclusion

Prediction rule ensembles can be a powerful tool for systematically exploring potential nuances in experimental treatment effects. By combining two core machine learning approaches and adhering to best practices regarding held-out estimation, we are able to quantify not only how treatment effects might vary in ways that are generalizable to new data but how useful identifying such variation is in predicting outcomes in that new data.

7 Causal Random Forests

In the previous section, we demonstrated how to use prediction rule ensembles to systematically identify heterogeneous treatment effects in one's experimental data that use out-of-sample prediction to reliably assess performance. Here, we demonstrate a different tree-based algorithm, the causal random forest, that can be used for similar purposes.[8]

The causal random forest is an extension of the commonly used random forest algorithm (Breiman 2001) discussed in Section 4. However, this extension has two distinctive characteristics that differentiate it from standard random forests: It is *causal* and it is *honest*; we explain what these terms mean in this context in Sections 7.1 and 7.2. We stick to a high-level, conceptual description here but invite you to read some of its foundational papers (Athey and Imbens 2016; Wager and Athey 2018; Athey, Tibshirani, and Wager 2019) for more detail regarding how it works.

---

[8] Some portions of this section are adapted from a blog post one of us (Mark) wrote in 2018: www .markhw.com/blog/causalforestintro.

The causal random forest has key features that make it particularly attractive for experimental research. First, the causal random forest allows for the estimation of standard errors around the point estimates of individual-level treatment effects, which can be especially useful for characterizing treatment effect heterogeneity. Second, and perhaps more importantly, the method is explicitly optimized on treatment effects, not outcomes. That is, instead of predicting Y_i for each individual, it predicts the difference we'd expect to see in Y_i between experimental conditions for that individual. This is a departure from traditional supervised learning algorithms, which focus on predicting the outcome itself. When applying such models to experimental data, treatment assignment and its potential interactions with other covariates are considered on equal footing with other features in the model (prediction rule ensembles, covered in Section 6, are one such example). As Blackwell and Olson (2022b) point out, this creates the potential for *indirect regularization bias*, which occurs when optimization for predicting the outcome itself leads machine learning methods to overregularize features important for characterizing moderating relationships between treatment and outcome (see also Ratkovic 2021).

7.1 What Makes It Causal?

Up until now, we have focused on methods that estimate an outcome, Y, as a function of some treatment, W, that is potentially moderated by some additional covariates, X. The first thing that differentiates the causal random forest from these previously discussed methods, including both the traditional random forest and the prediction rule ensembles discussed in the previous section, is that it does not estimate Y directly.

Instead, each tree explicitly searches for the subgroups where the treatment effects differ most. When we say "explicitly," we mean that it is baked into the criteria the tree uses to determine where to make splits. A typical regression tree might split the data by asking, "What variable and value would reduce the MSE the most if we made a split at that value of that variable?" In doing so, the typical tree predicts Y. But here we are less interested in predicting Y for that individual than we are in predicting the *treatment effect* for that individual. Therefore, we want to split the data by instead asking "What variable and value would maximize the difference in mean outcomes between treatment and control groups if we split at that value of that variable?"

The resulting decision tree gives us the difference in between the treatment and control conditions for each of its terminal nodes, or "leaves," representing an array of conditional average treatment effects. That the causal random forest explicitly estimates, and thereby optimizes for, conditional average treatment effects is one reason why it is often preferred for estimating treatment effect heterogeneity in experimental research. When a learner targets the outcome itself, it may focus too heavily on covariates that explain variation in the outcome but not variation in the treatment's effect on the outcome (Ratkovic 2021; Blackwell and Olson 2022b). When one is explicitly interested in how treatment effects vary by subgroup, it can be helpful to use a learner explicitly optimized for that purpose.

7.2 What Makes It Honest?

As with all other machine learning models, a primary concern is to avoid overfitting on this causal splitting criteria. The causal random forest guards against overfitting by enforcing an *honesty* condition that is satisfied when, for each decision tree, an observation is used for either splitting or estimating but not both (Wager and Athey 2018).

Specifically, each iteration of the algorithm takes the training data and randomly divides them into two subsamples: a splitting subsample and an estimating subsample. The splitting criteria described in Section 7.1 are applied to the splitting subsample, which builds us our tree of conditional average treatment effects. The rules identified in this tree are then applied to observations in the estimating subsample. That is, for a given tree, the actual estimated predictions from that tree are based on observations that were not used to determine how to split that tree. The treatment effect within each leaf – that is, the conditional average treatment effect for each terminal node of the tree – is determined as the difference between the mean of the treatment and the mean of the control cases for observations in the estimating subsample. That splitting and estimating are done on different data is one of the reasons we can obtain valid confidence intervals.

This might be difficult to follow, so we illustrate how this might play out in a simple real-world scenario (Figure 6), but note that the causal random forest would fit many of these trees and average across them.

Athey and colleagues have shown that these treatment effect estimates are asymptotically normal. This means that, over repeated sampling, the treatment effect estimates are normally distributed. In the eyes of some theoretical statisticians and academics, this is perhaps the biggest contribution of this approach. Practically, this means that we can calculate uncertainty intervals around our predicted treatment effects at the group or even individual level. Setting aside the well-documented problems with p-values and null hypothesis significance testing, this is very useful for an experimental social scientist because it allows us to appreciate the inherent uncertainty in our predictions.

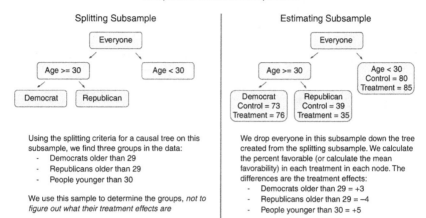

Figure 6 Causal forest splitting and estimating procedure

7.3 A Worked Example

Let's return to the data we used in the previous section: our experiment that asked likely Democratic primary voters to select between two hypothetical candidates with randomly generated characteristics, focusing on matchups that featured a male versus female candidate.

7.3.1 Code

As in Section 6.2.1, the code used to clean and preprocess the raw data for our purposes is included in the full replication materials.

We begin the code included here at the point where we shape our data in a way that the **grf** package will be able to use (Tibshirani et al. 2021). This means defining our outcome variable, Y (in this case, a binary indicator for whether the respondent preferred Candidate A over Candidate B), a binary treatment indicator, W (in this case, whether Candidate A was a woman), and our covariates, X, which are *one-hot encoded*. One-hot encoding transforms categorical variables in our data, such as the respondents' race, to binary variables representing each level of the respective categorical variable. Many regression packages do something similar implicitly; here, we are simply making that step explicit.

```
# Packages this code uses
library(grf)
library(data.table)
library(mltools)
library(tidyverse)
```

```
# Define outcome and treatment as binary vectors
Y <- as.numeric(df$picked_cand_a == TRUE)
W <- as.numeric(df$cand_a_female == TRUE)

# Define other independent variables as one-hot encoded data table
X <-
    # mltools::one_hot() takes a data.table object instead of a tidy
    object
    mltools::one_hot(
        data.table::data.table(
            df %>%
                # Remember to remove treatment and outcome from X!
                dplyr::select(-cand_a_female, -picked_cand_a)
        )
    )
```

We then, as always, set a seed and split our data into a training and testing set.

```
set.seed(1839)

# Identify cases to be used for training and testing
    # Training cases: random sample of 75% of observations in df
cases <- sample(seq_len(nrow(df)), round(nrow(df) * .75))

# Split X, Y, and W separately by cases indices
train_X <- X[cases, ]
test_X <- X[-cases, ]

train_Y = Y[cases]
test_Y = Y[-cases]

train_W = W[cases]
test_W = W[-cases]
```

Now we are ready to train our causal random forest. Note here that we estimated more than the default 2,000 trees. Additional hyperparameters common to tree-based learners can be specified, and we encourage readers to examine the package's help files (such as by running **?grf::causal_forest** in your R console) before using the function themselves.

```
# Train Model 1
m1 <- grf::causal_forest(

    # Define Y, X, and W
    Y = train_Y,
    X = train_X,
    W = train_W,
```

```
# Run more trees than default
num.trees = 5000,

# grf allows you to set a seed internally
seed = 1839
)
```

Model in hand, we can then predict treatment effects in our test set.

```
# Make individual level treatment effect predictions on test set
priority.cate <- predict(
    object = m1,
    newdata = test_X,

    # Optional, estimate variance if you want uncertainty intervals
    estimate.variance = TRUE
)
test_X$preds <- priority.cate$predictions
test_X$Y <- test_Y
test_X$W <- test_W
```

The first thing to check is the overall distribution of predicted effects (Figure 7). These predicted individual-level effects are sometimes referred to as *lift scores*, referring to how sensitive we expect each individual to be to our experimental treatment. This will give us a general sense of the extent to which there is variation relative to the overall average treatment effect.

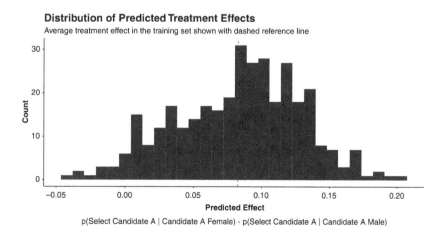

Figure 7 Distribution of predicted effects

```
test_X %>%
  ggplot(aes(x = preds)) +
  geom_histogram() +

  # Include training set naive difference in means for baseline
  geom_vline(
    xintercept = mean(train_Y[train_W == 1]) - mean(train_
Y[train_W == 0]),
    col = "red",
    lty = "dashed"
  ) +
  labs(
    title = "Distribution of Predicted Treatment Effects",
    subtitle = "Average treatment effect in the training set
shown with dashed reference line",
    y = "Count",
    x = "Predicted Effect\np(Select Candidate A | Candidate
A Female) - p(Select Candidate A | Candidate A Male)"
  ) +
  theme_book()
```

The distribution is single-peaked around the overall average treatment effect. Some respondents are predicted to be more or less sensitive to candidate gender, but what we do *not* see is a bimodal distribution where a large group of respondents is predicted to respond to female candidates less positively than the average while another group responds to them more positively than the average. Very few respondents, on the tails of the distribution, have predicted effects that are well above or below the average (a few fall slightly below zero).

We can examine this in more detail by plotting our uncertainty at the individual level. Recall that the predicted effects estimated by the generalized random forest are asymptotically normal, allowing us to calculate confidence intervals around our point estimates. Here, we can see that even though point estimates exhibit a large degree of variation, very few respondents – about as many as we'd expect by chance – are predicted to see effects that we'd call statistically significant at $p < 0.05$ (Figure 8).

```
# Plot predictions by their rank-order
ggplot(mapping = aes(
  x = data.table::frankv(preds$predictions, order = -1),
  y = preds$predictions
)) +
  geom_point() +
```

```
# Add uncertainty interval
geom_errorbar (mapping = aes (
    ymin = preds$predictions + 1.96 * sqrt (preds$variance.
estimates),
    ymax = preds$predictions - 1.96 * sqrt (preds$variance.
estimates)
)) +
geom_hline (yintercept = 0, col = "black") +

# Include training set naive difference in means for reference
geom_hline (
    yintercept = mean (train_Y[train_W == 1]) - mean (train_
Y[train_W == 0]),
    lty = "dashed",
    col = "red"
) +
labs (
    x = "Rank",
    y = "Estimated Treatment Effect",
    title = "Predicted Effects",
    subtitle = "Estimate and 95% uncertainty interval",
    caption = "Training set average treatment effect shown with
dashed red line"
) +
theme_book ()
```

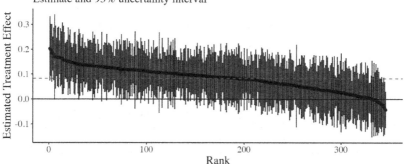

Figure 8 Individual effects with uncertainty

7.4 Is Our Heterogeneity Significant?

There are multiple reasons why we might not observe individual-level predictions that are statistically distinguishable from the overall average, ranging from a lack of statistical power to the inherent complexity of individuals. That is, an individual's predicted treatment effect bundles effects associated with each of their characteristics together. Many of these effects may be offsetting with respect to their divergence from the overall average. This means that even if we don't observe significant individual-level heterogeneity, individuals with differing predicted effects, and groups at higher levels of aggregation, may still tend to exhibit differential sensitivity to treatment.

7.4.1 A Simple Test

The first thing we can do to check that our predicted effects are in fact useful in this manner is to test whether they moderate the treatment effect in the test set. By which we mean, we can check whether respondents with higher predicted treatment effects *based on the model we fit on the training set* are in fact more likely to prefer female hypothetical candidates in our held-out data. We can do this with a simple linear regression, interacting actual treatment assignment with predicted treatment effects (z-scoring them to make the coefficients more interpretable).

```
# Does predicted heterogeneity moderate treatment effects in
the test set?
confirmatory <- lm(Y ~ W * scale(preds),
                   data = test_X)
```

The results show that respondents predicted to exhibit stronger preferences for female candidates are in fact significantly more likely to select Candidate A when Candidate A is a woman, and less likely to do so when Candidate A is a man, compared to respondents with weaker predicted effects (Table 8). This supports the idea that the causal random forest fit to our training data is useful for predicting treatment effect heterogeneity in our held-out data.

Table 8 Held-out heterogeneity by predicted heterogeneity

Term	Estimate	Standard Error	Statistic	*p*-value
(Intercept)	0.452	0.037	12.100	0.000
W	0.152	0.052	2.904	0.004
scale(preds)	−0.148	0.039	−3.783	0.000
W:scale(preds)	0.186	0.053	3.544	0.000

7.4.2 A More Formal Test

In addition to this simple diagnostic, we can formally test whether predicted individual effects are picking up treatment effect heterogeneity based on whether they offer a useful *prioritization* of individuals in the held-out data.

To do this, we estimate rank-weighted average treatment effects (RATEs), which can be implemented within **grf**. Described in greater detail in Yadlowsky et al. (2021), the RATE identifies how well a given prioritization rule – such as the predicted treatment effects produced by the causal random forest – performs in identifying the units in held-out data that will be most responsive to treatment.

In order to estimate the RATE, we first re-specify our causal forest on our held-out data. We then supply this model and predicted individual effects in the same data using the original model to **grf's rank_average_treatment_effect()** function. Note that there are two different options within this function for how to go about estimating the RATE. The first (default) uses the area under the total operating characteristic (AUTOC) curve; the second (which we use here) uses the Qini coefficient. Without going into too many details,[9] the first is a statistic that incorporates information from each quadrant of the true/false, positive/negative predictions generated by a model as one progressively decreases the probability threshold for predicting a positive case; the second evaluates the cumulative benefits of treating an increasing proportion of observations, sorted by their lift score. Both use bootstrapping to test whether their respective RATE estimates are statistically distinguishable from zero. Each can also be compared against the fit generated by a baseline prioritization that does not consider treatment assignment, though this is less applicable in our case where the baseline risk (i.e., probability of observing the outcome – picking Candidate A – independent of treatment assignment) is roughly equal for all respondents.

We chose to use the Qini coefficient as our target here because it gives symmetric weight to units with the highest and lowest scores, while the AUTOC will more strongly upweight observations with the highest scores. The AUTOC is most useful when one intends to prioritize a smaller number of units for treatment, and the question is which units will benefit the most from a targeted intervention. Here, we are estimating the effects of candidate gender, which cannot be "targeted" in the same sense (i.e., for a given election, the Democratic Party cannot nominate a woman for some voters and a man for others). Therefore, we evaluate our model performance here using the target

---

[9] See Yadlowsky et al. (2021) for extended discussion of these and other related metrics.

with symmetric weights. In your own applications, you will need to think through which metric is more appropriate based on your data and research question.

```
# Specify causal forest on the test (evaluation) set
m1_eval <- grf::causal_forest(
  Y = test_Y,
  X = test_X %>%
    # remove columns we previously added to test_X
    dplyr::select(-preds, -Y, -W),
  W = test_W,
  num.trees = 5000,
  seed = 1839
)

# compute RATE
# we're using QINI here, but can specify AUTOC instead
rate <- grf::rank_average_treatment_effect(
  forest = m1_eval,
  priorities = priority.cate$predictions,
  target = "QINI",
)
```

Depending on your application, it may also make sense to compare this estimated RATE to one that would be observed by setting priority for treatment using baseline risk. This is less applicable in our case because baseline risk is roughly equal for all respondents. However, in other survey experimental contexts, this will not be the case. For, example, when testing for heterogeneity in the effectiveness of messages to promote vaccination, it may be useful to compare the prioritization suggested by your model against a prioritization based on the probability of not already intending to take the vaccine in question.

```
# Compute a prioritization based on baseline risk
# This predicts the outcome as a function of independent variables,
    # in the control condition
rf.risk <- regression_forest(X[cases,] [W[cases] == 0, ],
                              Y[cases] [W[cases] == 0])
priority.risk <- predict(rf.risk, X[-cases,]) $predictions

# Test if two RATEs are equal
rate.diff <- rank_average_treatment_effect(m1_eval,
                  # comparing two prioritization rules
                  # with and without considering treatment
                          cbind(priority.cate$predictions,
                                priority.risk))
```

Table 9 RATE test for significant heterogeneity

Target	Esimate	Lower	Upper
V1 | QINI	0.050	0.020	0.080
priority.risk | QINI	-0.064	-0.092	-0.036
V1 – priority.risk | QINI	0.114	0.060	0.168

We can then generate estimates and uncertainty intervals for three quantities: the RATE of our model (V1 | QINI), the RATE of our baseline risk score (priority.risk | QINI), and the difference between these two (V1 – priority.risk | QINI). Here, it is less interesting that the RATE from our model is significantly higher than the RATE from our baseline risk score because the variation in baseline risk is trivial. However, we also see that our overall estimate of the RATE is positive and statistically significant (Table 9). Essentially, this tells us that the individual-level variation described by the causal random forest is useful for predicting treatment effects in the held-out data.

```
# construct uncertainty
rate.diff.table <- data.frame(
   Target = rate.diff$target,
   Esimate = rate.diff$estimate,
   Lower = rate.diff$estimate - 1.96 * rate.diff$std.err,
   Upper = rate.diff$estimate + 1.96 * rate.diff$std.err
)
```

7.5 Sources of Heterogeneity

Finally, we can examine the source of this heterogeneity by identifying the most important variables in the model. Recall from Section 6.2.1 that variable importance can mean different things for different tree-based models. Here, variable importance is represented as a weighted frequency of how often a given variable was selected for splitting the data – with higher weight given when the variable was used earlier in the tree. Essentially, the more important a variable is, the more often it offered the largest conditional average treatment effects in the splitting samples.

```
# Get ten most important variables
m1 %>%
   variable_importance() %>%
   as.data.frame() %>%
   mutate(Variable = colnames(m1$X.orig),
          V1 = round(V1, 3)) %>%
```

```
arrange(desc(V1)) %>%
rename(Importance = V1) %>%
slice(1:10) %>%
knitr::kable(format = "pipe", caption = "Variable Importance",
             label = "grf_importance")
```

Here, we see that variables such as respondents' age, favorability toward the #MeToo movement, and number of real-world female candidates they were considering voting for at the time emerge as most informative of predicted treatment effects (Table 10). However, it is important to note that none of these variable importances are overwhelming – all are less than 0.1.

There are a few reasons why this could be. First, it could be that there isn't much heterogeneity in the data. If there really aren't individual-level differences in predicted treatment effects, there won't be any variables that are useful for predicting such differences. However, it is also the case that many variable importance measures in random forest models, including this one, have important limitations that researchers must keep in mind when interpreting them (Strobl et al. 2007; Strobl et al. 2008). First, such measures can be vulnerable to collinearity: When multiple variables used to estimate the model contain similar information, they will be forced to "share" that information's importance. This could happen here if, for instance, younger respondents tend to hold more favorable attitudes toward the #MeToo movement. Second, continuous variables such as age can receive inflated importance, relative to binary variables, because there is more variation along which the algorithm can search for an ideal split. While this is not to say that you should completely ignore variable

Table 10 Variable importance

Importance	Variable
0.091	age
0.075	favmetoo
0.063	considerwoman_n
0.057	sdo
0.049	progressive
0.045	horserace_Warren
0.038	gender
0.034	candwarm
0.033	considerwoman
0.033	horserace_Biden

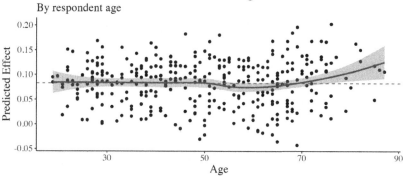

Figure 9 Effects by age

importance measures when using tree-based methods, this is to encourage caution when interpreting them.

Take, for example, age – the variable given the highest importance in this model. Despite its high importance, it is not obvious from examining the relationship between age and predicted effects how the effect varies along this dimension (Figure 9). For all but the oldest respondents, predicted effects are as likely to be above the overall average as the lower – and by similar amounts.

This is not the case for the next most important variable, favorability toward the #MeToo movement. The distribution of predicted effects among respondents who hold unfavorable views toward the #MeToo movement are clearly centered around a lower value than the corresponding distribution among respondents with a favorable view (Figure 10). That is, it may be safer to say that there is meaningful heterogeneity along this dimension. While most of the respondents in the data hold favorable opinions toward the #MeToo movement, those who hold unfavorable opinions toward it also hold weaker preferences for women over men in our hypothetical candidate matchups.

It is important to clarify that distributions of predicted individual-level effects broken out by some characteristic are *different* than the conditional average treatment effects associated with that characteristic. Individuals with unfavorable views toward the #MeToo movement may differ from those with favorable views along a variety of other characteristics that are associated with these treatment effects, so the plot in Figure 10 is not isolating the conditional effects of #MeToo favorability itself as we might by specifying a single interaction term in a linear model.

Predicted Effect of Candidate Being a Woman

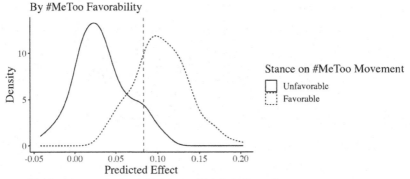

Figure 10 Distribution of predicted effects by #MeToo attitudes

7.6 Conclusion

We have demonstrated how to implement the causal random forest and conduct basic analyses of its output at the individual, group, and variable levels. We note that researchers are likely to find the causal random forest to be especially useful for estimating treatment effect heterogeneity because it was explicitly designed for that purpose, allows for the prediction of individual-level treatment effects, and builds held-out, "honest" estimation directly into the algorithm. We do caution readers against overinterpreting measures of variable importance and to take care when moving from predicted individual-level effects that bundle the effects of many characteristics into one estimate to group-level differences attributable to a single characteristic. Finally, even when using methods that build in honest estimation "under the hood," we still strongly encourage users to validate the presence of treatment effect heterogeneity using a dedicated held-out sample, which bolsters evidence for a replicable pattern in the data.

8 Conclusion

We began by discussing causal inference within the potential outcomes frame-work, where we can think of people having outcomes had they been in condition 1 and also had they been in condition 2. We can only observe one of these two potential outcomes, which is the fundamental problem of causal inference. We discussed how randomized experiments are a great tool at getting an average treatment effect in this context.

We then spent the next two sections discussing the replication "crisis" in social science and the basics of machine learning. In the last fifteen years, there has been increasing concern that published findings in the literature are not replicable – when others try to do the same study, they do not get the same results. This has led to some proposals such as pre-registration, where researchers indicate their hypotheses and exactly what they will do ahead of time. This may limit science by discouraging exploratory analyses, which can lead to new discoveries. We introduced the basic concepts of machine learning, focusing on how the methods are aimed at making useful predictions and rely on techniques like penalization, ensembles, and cross-validation to make sure that we do not overfit a model to the present data.

We then brought these concepts together with theoretical and practical introductions to using machine learning to estimate heterogeneous treatment effects, specifically demonstrating prediction rule ensembles and the causal random forest. These methods explore potential interactions in the data while using approaches from machine learning to reduce the likelihood that any relationships we identify are unique to our specific dataset and instead represent generalizable and replicable social phenomena. We provided a conceptual overview and R tutorials for each of these methods that researchers can use to examine treatment effect heterogeneity in their own work.

This brings us back to the two goals we had for the Element. First, we hope that the specific knowledge about how to implement these methods gives the reader the tools they need to use these methods in their own research. But this is an active area of methodological development, and we have demonstrated just two of many currently available methods in this area, to say nothing of the rapidly expanding set of available methods in this emerging field. And so, second, we hope that the description of potential outcomes, machine learning concepts, and heterogeneous treatment effects equips the reader with the requisite background to be able to learn new technologies as they arise and are turned into widely available statistical software.

However, these methods are not a panacea. Here, we discuss several limitations of these methods before providing a range of other related methods that are currently available and implemented in R.

8.1 Limitations and Potential Abuses

Now that we have demonstrated how to use some of these methods and why they are useful, it is important to emphasize some limitations of these methods such that researchers can avoid abusing them.

First, we argued that the methods proposed here can help researchers perform exploratory data analysis in a principled way. This does not mean that these methods generate results that are always reproduced in future replications.

These are probabilistic models that assume a constant data generating process. This assumption may be violated by the nature of social science: The phenomena we study can change quickly. So there will still be Type I errors in the sense that a LASSO penalty might not shrink the coefficient of a variable to zero that should rightly be zero. And there will be Type II errors in that an ensemble may underestimate the true role of a variable in predicting an outcome.

What we mean by "principled" is that these methods offer procedures for exploring data that are not determined by the whims and motivations of a researcher, who may selectively choose interactions and covariates until a desired outcome has a p-value lower than 0.05. Indeed, machine learning methods are not a substitute for other best practices for reproducible research, such as pre-registration. It is still useful – even if the research question is fundamentally exploratory – to record researcher-determined decisions such as which covariates will be considered, how they will be preprocessed, how hyperparameters will be tuned, and so on before performing analyses. That is, you can always specify a procedure in advance even in the absence of formal hypotheses. Relying on cross-validation and out-of-sample error helps us look for patterns that are likelier to be present in the true data generating process, but these methods are not infallible. Our focus is more on what machine learning can add to a researcher's toolkit and less on what it can replace.

Furthermore, we agree with Stieger (1990) that "*An ounce of replication is worth a ton of inferential statistics*" (p. 176, italics in original). These methods can be useful for exploring data. Researchers can use what they have found with prediction rule ensembles and causal random forests to inform future studies, seeking to replicate in wholly new samples relationships previously uncovered through cross-validation. That is, these methods can be as useful for theory generation as they are for theory testing.

Second, we note that one each of these methods is just that: one method, with its own procedures, goals, and assumptions. Careful readers will have noticed that while we consistently identified treatment effect heterogeneity in our candidate choice experiment using each of the methods we demonstrated, these methods indicated that different independent variables were important for characterizing that heterogeneity. Some of these differences are due to the different ways that these methods calculate variable "importance," and we cautioned against overinterpreting such variable importance metrics in Sections 6 and 7. However, these differences also highlight that these two methods differ in other fundamental ways (e.g., prediction rule ensembles limit tree depth by default so as to prioritize interpretability, while the causal random forest explicitly optimizes on conditional average treatment effects rather than the outcome itself). These differences are crucial to keep in mind when conducting research in this area, and it is often advisable to compare results (and out-of-sample performance) across multiple methods.

Finally, there is no free lunch here. Machine learning methods tend to require more data than traditional laboratory studies in the social sciences. In holding out data for estimation, especially with the causal forest, datasets should ideally be in the thousands of rows rather than the hundreds. This is costly to collect – but is also a reason why these methods are so important. Large datasets cost resources, and here we provide principled ways to explore these data such that strict pre-registration does not limit what we can learn from them.

8.2 Additional Methods

As we mentioned, heterogenous treatment effects methodology is an area under active development. Our hope is that this Element has acquainted you with the basic knowledge needed to explore methods that we did not cover in this Element. Many packages exist that are both (a) peer-reviewed and (b) on the Comprehensive R Archive Network (CRAN): **aVirtualTwins** (Foster, Taylor, and Ruberg 2011; Vieille and Foster 2018), **BART** and a companion package **tidytreatment** (Green and Kern 2012; Sparapani, Spanbauer, and McCulloch 2021; Bon 2022), **beanz** (Wang et al. 2018), **FindIt** (Imai and Ratkovic 2013), **GenericML** (Chernozhukov et al. 2018), **model4you** (Seibold, Zeileis, and Hothorn 2019), **personalized** (Chen et al. 2017; Huling and Yu 2021), **Quint** (Dusseldorp and Van Mechelen 2014; Dusseldorp, Doove, and Mechelen 2016), **SIDES** (Lipkovich et al. 2011; Riviere 2021), **subtee** (Ballarini et al. 2021), and **inters** (Blackwell and Olson 2022a).

With a sprawling collection of algorithms in the literature, some have tried to organize the literature and establish more generalized methods. Both the **personalized** and **GenericML** packages are part of this effort. The underlying approaches are *model agnostic* in that one can apply them in conjunction with any machine learning method: LASSO, random forest, boosted trees, and so on. Künzel et al. (2019) articulate general frameworks for calculating treatment effects, where the underlying models can be based on any machine learning algorithm (see also Nie and Wager 2021). These methods tend to involve creative ways of examining differences in predictions between treated and control units, with inferential statistics performed via bootstrapping or on a held-out dataset.

Künzel and colleagues articulate three types of learners: the S-learner, T-learner, and X-learner. In the S-learner, the first step is to fit any machine learning model to the data, including the treatment indicator as any other covariate used to predict the outcome. Then, one uses this model to generate predictions on two versions of the data: one where everyone is coded as having been treated and another where everyone is coded as having been in the control condition. The differences between these predictions – essentially individual-level marginal effects of treatment assignment – are taken as predicted treatment effects. This is precisely what the **BART/tidytreatment** approach does (see Green and Kern 2012); we can see that as not a uniquely specific algorithm but an example of an S-learner. The S in S-learner is short for "single," referring to the single machine learning model fit to the training data. This is in contrast to the T-leaner, short for "two" learner, which subsets on treatment assignment rather than including it as a covariate and therefore fits two models – one on treated units and one on control units. Finally, the X-learner averages predicted individual-level treatment effects from two parallel pipelines in which training and prediction occur on different subsets of the data in crosswise fashion. This framework is an example of how the literature is starting to form a coherent structure instead of a list of disparate algorithms.

8.3 Coda

We would like to thank you for reading through this Element on machine learning for experiments in the social sciences. We hope it has provided instructive tutorials and enough conceptual background that you can continue to discover new causal machine learning methods. This is a growing area of methodological development, and we hope that we've demystified an exciting field that might appear at first glance to be overly complicated from the perspective of someone who (like us) is trained in statistics and methodology in the social sciences.

References

Abramson, Scott F., Korhan Kocak, Asya Magazinnik, and Anton Strezhnev. 2020. "Improving Preference Elicitation in Conjoint Designs Using Machine Learning for Heterogeneous Effects." Working paper. www.korhankocak.com/publication/akms/.

Athey, Susan, and Guido Imbens. 2016. "Recursive Partitioning for Heterogeneous Causal Effects." *Proceedings of the National Academy of Sciences* 113 (27): 7353–7360.

Athey, Susan, Julie Tibshirani, and Stefan Wager. 2019. "Generalized Random Forests." *Annals of Statistics* 47 (2): 1148–1178.

Ballarini, Nicolas M., Marius Thomas, Gerd K. Rosenkranz, and Björn Bornkamp. 2021. "Subtee: An R Package for Subgroup Treatment Effect Estimation in Clinical Trials." *Journal of Statistical Software* 99 (14): 1–17.

Bates, Stephen, Trevor Hastie, and Robert Tibshirani. 2021. "Cross-Validation: What Does It Estimate and How Well Does It Do It?" Working paper. https://arxiv.org/abs/2104.00673.

Beebee, Helen, Christopher Hitchcock, and Peter Menzies. 2009. *The Oxford Handbook of Causation.* Oxford: Oxford University Press.

Beiser-McGrath, Janina, and Liam Beiser-McGrath. 2020. "Problems with Products? Control Strategies for Models with Interaction and Quadratic Effects." *Political Science Research and Methods* 8 (4): 707–730.

Blackwell, Matthew, and Michael Olson. 2022a. *Inters: Flexible Tools for Estimating Interactions.* https://CRAN.R-project.org/package=inters.

2022b. "Reducing Model Misspecification and Bias in the Estimation of Interactions." *Political Analysis* 30 (4): 495–514.

Blair, Elizabeth. 2020. "'Ugly,' 'Discordant': New Executive Order Takes Aim at Modern Architecture." *NPR*, December 21. www.npr.org/2020/02/13/805256707/just-plain-ugly-proposed-executive-order-takes-aim-at-modern-architecture.

Bon, Joshua J. 2022. *Tidytreatment: Tidy Methods for Bayesian Treatment Effect Models.* https://CRAN.R-project.org/package=tidytreatment.

Breiman, Leo. 1996. "Bagging Predictors." *Machine Learning* 24: 123–140.

2001. "Random Forests." *Machine Learning* 45: 5–32.

Bryan, Christopher J., Elizabeth Tipton, and David S. Yeager. 2021. "Behavioural Science Is Unlikely to Change the World without a Heterogeneity Revolution." *Nature Human Behavior* 5: 980–989.

Burkov, Andriy. 2019. *The Hundred-Page Machine Learning Book*. Andriy Burkov.

Campbell, Donald T. 1973. "The Social Scientist As Methodological Servant of the Experimenting Society." *Policy Studies and the Social Sciences* 2 (1): 27–32.

Chen, Shuai, Lu Tian, Tianxi Cai, and Menggang Yu. 2017. "A General Statistical Framework for Subgroup Identification and Comparative Treatment Scoring." *Biometrics* 73 (4): 1199–1209. https://doi.org/10.1111/biom.12676.

Chen, Tianqi, and Carlos Guestrin. 2016. "XGBoost: A Scalable Tree Boosting System." In *KDD '16: Proceedings of the 22nd ACM SIGKDD International Conference on Knowledge Discovery and Data Mining*, 785–794. New York: Association for Computing Machinery. https://doi.org/10.1145/2939672.2939785.

Chen, Tianqi, Tong He, Michael Benesty et al. 2022. *Xgboost: Extreme Gradient Boosting*. https://CRAN.R-project.org/package=xgboost.

Chernozhukov, Victor, Mert Demirer, Esther Duflo, and Ivan Fernandez-Val. 2018. "Generic Machine Learning Inference on Heterogeneous Treatment Effects in Randomized Experiments, with an Application to Immunization in India." National Bureau of Economic Research. Working Paper No. 24678.

Collaboration, Open Science. 2015. "Estimating the Reproducibility of Psychological Science." *Science* 349 (6251): aac4716.

Crandall, Christian S., Paul J. Silvia, Ahogni Nicolas N'Gbala, Jo-Ann Tsang, and Karen Dawson. 2007. "Balance Theory, Unit Relations, and Attribution: The Underlying Integrity of Heiderian Theory." *Review of General Psychology* 11 (1): 12–30.

Cranmer, Skyler, and Bruce Desmarais. 2017. "What Can We Learn from Predictive Modeling?" *Political Analysis* 25 (2): 145–166.

Cronbach, Lee J. 1975. "Beyond the Two Disciplines of Scientific Psychology." *American Psychologist* 30 (2): 116–127.

Dusseldorp, Elise, Lisa Doove, and Iven van Mechelen. 2016. "Quint: An R Package for the Identification of Subgroups of Clients Who Differ in Which Treatment Alternative Is Best for Them." *Behavior Research Methods* 48 (2): 650–663.

Dusseldorp, Elise, and Iven Van Mechelen. 2014. "Qualitative Interaction Trees: A Tool to Identify Qualitative Treatment–Subgroup Interactions." *Statistics in Medicine* 33 (2): 219–237.

Ebersole, Charles R., Olivia E. Atherton, Aimee L. Belanger et al. 2016. "Many Labs 3: Evaluating Participant Pool Quality across the Academic Semester via Replication." *Journal of Experimental Social Psychology* 67: 68–82.

Ebersole, Charles R., Maya B. Mathur, Erica Baranski et al. 2020. "Many Labs 5: Testing Pre-Data-Collection Peer Review As an Intervention to Increase Replicability." *Advances in Methods and Practices in Psychological Science* 3 (3): 309–331.

Fariss, Christopher, and Zachary Jones. 2018. "Enhancing Validity in Observational Settings When Replication Is Not Possible." *Political Science Research and Methods* 6 (2): 365–380.

Fokkema, Marjolein. 2020. "Fitting Prediction Rule Ensembles with R Package pre." *Journal of Statistical Software* 92 (12): 1–30.

Fokkema, Marjolein, and Carolin Strobl. 2020. "Fitting Prediction Rule Ensembles to Psychological Research Data: An Introduction and Tutorial." *Psychological Methods* 25 (5): 636–652.

Foster, Jared C., Jeremy M. G. Taylor, and Stephen J. Ruberg. 2011. "Subgroup Identification from Randomized Clinical Trial Data." *Statistics in Medicine* 30 (24): 2867–2880.

Freund, Yoav, and Robert E. Schapire. 1996. "Experiments with a New Boosting Algorithm." In Lorenza Saitta, ed., *ICML '96: Proceedings of the Thirteenth International Conference on Machine Learning*, 148–156. San Francisco, CA: Morgan Kaufmann.

Friedman, Jerome. 2002. "Stochastic Gradient Boosting." *Computational Statistics and Data Analysis* 38 (4): 367–378.

Gelman, Andrew. 2015. "The Connection between Varying Treatment Effects and the Crisis of Unreplicable Research: A Bayesian Perspective." *Journal of Management* 41 (2): 632–643.

Gelman, Andrew, and Eric Loken. 2013. "The Garden of Forking Paths: Why Multiple Comparisons Can Be a Problem, Even When There Is No 'Fishing Expedition' or 'P-Hacking' and the Research Hypothesis Was Posited Ahead of Time." [Online]. www.stat.columbia.edu/~gelman/research/unpublished/p_hacking.pdf.

Gentzkow, Matthew, Shapiro Jesse, and Matthew Taddy. 2019. "Measuring Group Differences in High Dimensional Choices: Method and Application to Congressional Speech." *Econometrica* 87 (4): 1307–1340.

Géron, Aurélien. 2019. *Hands-On Machine Learning with Scikit-Learn, Keras, and Tensorflow: Concepts, Tools, and Techniques to Build Intelligent Systems*. Sebastopol, CA: O'Reilly Media.

Glass, Gene V. 1976. "Primary, Secondary, and Meta-Analysis of Research." *Educational Researcher* 5 (10): 3–8.

Green, Donald, and Holger Kern. 2012. "Modeling Heterogeneous Treatment Effects in Survey Experiments with Bayesian Additive Regression Trees." *Public Opinion Quarterly* 76 (3): 491–511.

Green, Donald P., and Alan S. Gerber. 2004. *Get Out the Vote! How to Increase Voter Turnout*. Washington, DC: Brookings Institution Press.

Green, Jon, Brian Schaffner, and Sam Luks. 2023. "Strategic Discrimination in the 2020 Democratic Primary." *Public Opinion Quarterly* nfac051. https://doi.org/10.1093/poq/nfac051.

Grimmer, Justin, Solomon Messing, and Sean J. Westwood. 2017. "Estimating Heterogeneous Treatment Effects and the Effects of Heterogeneous Treatments with Ensemble Methods." *Political Analysis* 25 (4): 413–434.

Ham, Dae Woong, Kosuke Imai, and Lucas Janson. 2022. "Using Machine Learning to Test Causal Hypotheses in Conjoint Analysis." arXiv. https://arxiv.org/abs/2201.08343.

Hare, Christopher, and Mikayla Kutsuris. 2022. "Measuring Swing Voters with a Supervised Machine Learning Ensemble." *Political Analysis*, 1–17. www.cambridge.org/core/journals/political-analysis/article/measuring-swing-voters-with-a-supervised-machine-learning-ensemble/145B1D6B0B2877FC454FBF446F9F1032.

Hastie, Trevor, Robert Tibshirani, and Jerome Friedman. 2009. *The Elements of Statistical Learning: Data Mining, Inference, and Prediction*. New York: Springer Science & Business Media.

Head, Megan L., Luke Holman, Rob Lanfear, Andrew T Kahn, and Michael D Jennions. 2015. "The Extent and Consequences of P-Hacking in Science." *PLoS Biology* 13 (3): e1002106.

Heider, Fritz. 1958. *The Psychology of Interpersonal Relations*. New York: Wiley.

Hernàn, Miguel A., and Tyler J. VanderWeele. 2011. "Compound Treatments and Transportability of Causal Inference." *Epidemiology* 22 (3): 368–377.

Hoffman, Jake M., Amit Sharma, and Duncan J. Watts. 2021. "Prediction and Explanation in Social Systems." *Science* 355 (6324): 486–488. https://science.sciencemag.org/content/355/6324/486.

Holland, Paul W. 1986. "Statistics and Causal Inference." *Journal of the American Statistical Association* 81 (396): 945–960.

Huling, Jared D., and Menggang Yu. 2021. "Subgroup Identification Using the personalized Package." *Journal of Statistical Software* 98 (5): 1–60. https://doi.org/10.18637/jss.v098.i05.

Imai, Kosuke, and Marc Ratkovic. 2013. "Estimating Treatment Effect Heterogeneity in Randomized Program Evaluation." *Annals of Applied Statistics* 7 (1): 443–470.

Imai, Kosuke, and Aaron Strauss. 2011. "Estimation of Heterogeneous Treatment Effects from Randomized Experiments, with Application to the Optimal Planning of the Get-Out-the-Vote Campaign." *Political Analysis* 19 (1): 1–19.

James, Gareth, Daniela Witten, Trevor Hastie, and Robert Tibshirani. 2013. *An Introduction to Statistical Learning*. New York: Springer.

Keele, Luke. 2015. "The Statistics of Causal Inference: A View from Political Methodology." *Political Analysis* 23 (3): 313–335.

Kerr, Norbert L. 1998. "HARKing: Hypothesizing After the Results Are Known." *Personality and Social Psychology Review* 2 (3): 196–217.

Klein, Richard A., Corey L. Cook, Charles R. Ebersole et al. 2019. "Many Labs 4: Failure to Replicate Mortality Salience Effect with and without Original Author Involvement." PsyArXiv. https://doi.org/10.31234/osf.io/vef2c.

Klein, Richard A., Michelangelo Vianello, Fred Hasselman et al. 2018. "Many Labs 2: Investigating Variation in Replicability across Samples and Settings." *Advances in Methods and Practices in Psychological Science* 1 (4): 443–490.

Kuhn, Max, and Kjell Johnson. 2013. *Applied Predictive Modeling*. Vol. 26. New York: Springer.

Kuhn, Max, and Julia Silge. 2022. *Tidy Modeling with R: A Framework for Modeling in the Tidyverse*. Sebastopol, CA: O'Reilly Media.

Künzel, Sören R., Jasjeet S. Sekhon, Peter J. Bickel, and Bin Yu. 2019. "Metalearners for Estimating Heterogeneous Treatment Effects Using Machine Learning." *Proceedings of the National Academy of Sciences* 116 (10): 4156–4165.

Lipkovich, Ilya, Alex Dmitrienko, Jonathan Denne, and Gregory Enas. 2011. "Subgroup Identification Based on Differential Effect Search: A Recursive Partitioning Method for Establishing Response to Treatment in Patient Subpopulations." *Statistics in Medicine* 30 (21): 2601–2621.

McClelland, Gary H., and Charles M. Judd. 1993. "Statistical Difficulties of Detecting Interactions and Moderator Effects." *Psychological Bulletin* 114 (2): 376.

Montgomery, Jacob M., and Santiago Olivella. 2018. "Tree-Based Models for Political Science Data." *American Journal of Political Science* 62 (3): 729–744.

Nicholson, Stephen. 2012. "Polarizing Cues." *American Journal of Political Science* 56 (1): 52–66.

Nicosia, Jessica, Emily R. Cohen-Shikora, and David A. Balota. 2021. "Re-examining Age Differences in the Stroop Effect: The Importance of the Trees in the Forest (Plot)." *Psychology and Aging* 36 (2): 214–231.

Nie, Xinkun, and Stefan Wager. 2021. "Quasi-Oracle Estimation of Heterogeneous Treatment Effects." *Biometrika* 108 (2): 299–319.

Nosek, Brian A., Charles R. Ebersole, Alexander C. DeHaven, and David T. Mellor. 2018. "The Preregistration Revolution." *Proceedings of the National Academy of Sciences* 115 (11): 2600–2606.

Peterson, Andrew, and Arthur Spirling. 2018. "Classification Accuracy As a Substantive Quantity of Interest: Measuring Polarization in Westminster Systems." *Political Analysis* 26 (1): 120–128.

Polley, Eric, Erin LeDell, Chris Kennedy, and Mark van der Laan. 2021. *SuperLearner: Super Learner Prediction.* https://CRAN.R-project.org/package=SuperLearner.

Ratkovic, Marc. 2021. "Subgroup Analysis: Pitfalls, Promise, and Honesty." In James N. Druckman and Donald P. Green (Eds.), *Advances in Experimental Political Science*, 271–288. Cambridge: Cambridge University Press. https://doi.org/10.1017/9781108777919.020.

Ratkovic, Marc, and Dustin Tingley. 2017. "Sparse Estimation and Uncertainty with Application to Subgroup Analysis." *Political Analysis* 25 (1): 1–40.

Ripley, Brian. 2021. *Tree: Classification and Regression Trees.* https://CRAN.R-project.org/package=tree.

Riviere, Marie-Karelle. 2021. *SIDES: Subgroup Identification Based on Differential Effect Search.* https://CRAN.R-project.org/package=SIDES.

Rosenthal, Robert. 1979. "The File Drawer Problem and Tolerance for Null Results." *Psychological Bulletin* 86 (3): 638.

Rubin, Donald B. 1974. "Estimating Causal Effects of Treatments in Randomized and Nonrandomized Studies." *Journal of Educational Psychology* 66 (5): 688–701.

2008. "For Objective Causal Inference, Design Trumps Analysis." *Annals of Applied Statistics* 2 (3): 808–840.

Rubin, Mark, and Chris Donkin. 2022. "Exploratory Hypothesis Tests Can Be More Compelling Than Confirmatory Hypothesis Tests." *Philosophical Psychology.* https://doi.org/10.1080/09515089.2022.2113771.

Seibold, Heidi, Achim Zeileis, and Torsten Hothorn. 2019. "Model4you: An R Package for Personalised Treatment Effect Estimation." *Journal of Open Research Software* 7 (1). http://doi.org/10.5334/jors.219.

Shmueli, Galit. 2010. "To Explain or to Predict?" *Statistical Science* 25 (3): 289–310.

Shrout, Patrick E., and Joseph L. Rodgers. 2018. "Psychology, Science, and Knowledge Construction: Broadening Perspectives from the Replication Crisis." *Annual Review of Psychology* 69 (1): 487–510. https://doi.org/10.1146/annurev-psych-122216-011845.

Silberzahn, Raphael, Eric L. Uhlmann, Daniel P. Martin et al. 2018. "Many Analysts, One Data Set: Making Transparent How Variations in Analytic

Choices Affect Results." *Advances in Methods and Practices in Psychological Science* 1 (3): 337–356.

Simmons, Joseph P., Leif D. Nelson, and Uri Simonsohn. 2011. "False-Positive Psychology: Undisclosed Flexibility in Data Collection and Analysis Allows Presenting Anything As Significant." *Psychological Science* 22 (11): 1359–1366.

Simonsohn, Uri, Leif D. Nelson, and Joseph P. Simmons. 2014. "P-Curve: A Key to the File-Drawer." *Journal of Experimental Psychology: General* 143 (2): 534.

Soderberg, Courtney K., Timothy M. Errington, Sarah R. Schiavone et al. 2021. "Initial Evidence of Research Quality of Registered Reports Compared with the Standard Publishing Model." *Nature Human Behaviour* 5: 990–997. https://doi.org/10.1038/s41562-021-01142-4.

Sparapani, Rodney, Charles Spanbauer, and Robert McCulloch. 2021. "Nonparametric Machine Learning and Efficient Computation with Bayesian Additive Regression Trees: The BART R Package." *Journal of Statistical Software* 97 (1): 1–66. https://doi.org/10.18637/jss.v097.i01.

Stieger, James H. 1990. "Structural Model Evaluation and Modification: An Interval Estimation Approach." *Multivariate Behavioral Research* 25 (2): 173–180.

Strobl, Carolin, Anne-Laure Boulesteix, Thomas Kneib, Thomas Augustin, and Achim Zeileis. 2008. "Conditional Variable Importance for Random Forests." *BMC Bioinformatics* 9 (307). https://doi.org/10.1186/1471-2105-9-307.

Strobl, Carolin, Anne-Laure Boulesteix, Achim Zeileis, and Torsten Hothorn. 2007. "Bias in Random Forest Variable Importance Measures: Illustrations, Sources and a Solution." *BMC Bioinformatics* 8 (25). https://doi.org/10.1186/1471-2105-8-25.

Tibshirani, Julie, Susan Athey, Erik Sverdrup, and Stefan Wager. 2021. *Grf: Generalized Random Forests.* https://CRAN.R-project.org/package=grf.

Vieille, Francois, and Jared Foster. 2018. *AVirtualTwins: Adaptation of Virtual Twins Method from Jared Foster.* https://CRAN.R-project.org/package=aVirtualTwins.

Wager, Stefan, and Susan Athey. 2018. "Estimation and Inference of Heterogeneous Treatment Effects Using Random Forests." *Journal of the American Statistical Association* 113 (523): 1228–1242.

Wang, Chenguang, Thomas A. Louis, Nicholas C. Henderson, Carlos O. Weiss, and Ravi Varadhan. 2018. "Beanz: An R Package for Bayesian Analysis of Heterogeneous Treatment Effects with a Graphical User Interface." *Journal of Statistical Software* 85 (7): 1–31.

Wright, Marvin N., and Andreas Ziegler. 2017. "ranger: A Fast Implementation of Random Forests for High Dimensional Data in C++ and R." *Journal of Statistical Software* 77 (1): 1–17. https://doi.org/10.18637/jss.v077.i01.

Yadlowsky, Steve, Scott Fleming, Nigam Shah, Emma Brunskill, and Stefan Wager. 2021. "Evaluating Treatment Prioritization Rules via Rank-Weighted Average Treatment Effects." arXiv. https://arxiv.org/abs/2111.07966.

Yarkoni, Tal, and Jacob Westfall. 2017. "Choosing Prediction over Explanation in Psychology: Lessons from Machine Learning." Perspectives on Psychological Science 12 (6): 1100–1122.

Acknowledgments

We thank Pablo Crespo, Nic Fishman, Kristin Lunz Trujillo, and two anonymous reviewers for helpful feedback on earlier drafts of this Element.

Cambridge Elements ≡

Experimental Political Science

James N. Druckman
Northwestern University

James N. Druckman is the Payson S. Wild Professor of Political Science and the Associate Director of the Institute for Policy Research at Northwestern University. He served as an editor for the journals Political Psychology and Public Opinion Quarterly as well as the University of Chicago Press's series in American Politics. He currently is the co-Principal Investigator of Time-Sharing Experiments for the Social Sciences (TESS) and sits on the American National Election Studies' Board. He previously served as President of the American Political Science Association section on Experimental Research and helped oversee the launching of the Journal of Experimental Political Science. He was co-editor of the Cambridge Handbook of Experimental Political Science. He is a Fellow of the American Academy of Arts and Sciences and has published more than 100 articles/book chapters on public opinion, political communication, campaigns, research methods, and other topics.

About the Series

There currently are few outlets for extended works on experimental methodology in political science. The new Experimental Political Science Cambridge Elements series features research on experimental approaches to a given substantive topic, and experimental methods by prominent and upcoming experts in the field.

Printed in the United States
by Baker & Taylor Publisher Services